Zvol set

Da Capo Press Series in
ARCHITECTURE AND DECORATIVE ART
General Editor: Adolf K. Placzek
Avery Librarian, Columbia University

41

EARLY VICTORIAN ARCHITECTURE
IN BRITAIN

YALE HISTORICAL PUBLICATIONS

George Kubler, Editor

History of Art: 9

The publication of the first edition of this work was aided

by funds provided by the Yale Department of the History of Art

deriving from a bequest of Isabel Paul.

EARLY VICTORIAN

ARCHITECTURE

IN BRITAIN

by Henry-Russell Hitchcock

Volume 2: Illustrations

DA CAPO PRESS • NEW YORK • 1972

Library of Congress Cataloging in Publication Data

Hitchcock, Henry Russell, 1903-
    Early Victorian architecture in Britain.
    (Da Capo Press series in architecture and decorative
art, 41)
    Original ed. issued as no. 9 of Yale historical publica-
tions. History of art.
    CONTENTS: v. 1. Text.—v. 2. Illustrations.
1. Architecture—Great Britain. 2. Architecture,
Victorian—Great Britain. I. Title. II. Series:
Yale historical publications. History of art, 9.
[NA967.H55   1972]   720'.942   72-151765
ISBN 0-306-70195-2

First published, 1954, by Yale University Press, New Haven,
Connecticut; reprinted, 1972, through special arrangement
with Yale University Press and, for the British market, with
The Architectural Press Ltd., London.

Copyright, 1954, by Yale University Press

Printed in the United States of America by the Meriden
Gravure Company, Meriden, Connecticut

Published by Da Capo Press, Inc.
A Subsidiary of Plenum Publishing Corporation
227 West 17th Street, New York, New York 10011

ILLUSTRATIONS

I 1   Westminster New Palace, London. By Sir Charles Barry, A. N. W. Pugin, and E. M. Barry. Original design 1835–36; executed 1840–c.1865. Photo. *Picture Post.*

I 2   Athenaeum, Mosley St., Manchester. By Sir Charles Barry, (1836) 1837–39. Photo. National Buildings Record.

I 3   Original design for Athenaeum, Manchester. By Sir Charles Barry, 1836. From *Surveyor, Engineer and Architect,* 1843.

I 4   St. Mary's, Southwark, London. By Benjamin Ferrey, 1840–41. From Companion to the *British Almanac,* 1842.

I 5   St. Agatha's, Llanymynech, Shropshire. By R. K. Penson, 1842–44. From *Illustrated London News,* 21 Sept. 1844.

I 6   Design for "Swiss Chalet." From P. F. Robinson, *Designs for Ornamental Villas,* 1827.

I 7   Highclere Castle, near Burghclere, Hampshire. As refaced by Sir Charles Barry, (1837) 1842–c.1855. From *Building News,* 1 Jan. 1858.

I 8   Travellers' Club House, Pall Mall, London. By Sir Charles Barry, (1829) 1830–32. Elevation from W. H. Leeds, *The Travellers' Club House,* 1839.

I 9   Harlaxton Hall, near Grantham. By Anthony Salvin, 1834–c.1855. Photo. *Country Life.*

II 1   Design for "Pleasure Cottage." Elevation and plan from James Malton, *An Essay on British Cottage Architecture,* 1798.

II 2   Design for "Rustic Double Cottage." Elevation and plan from Sir John Soane, *Sketches in Architecture,* 1798.

II 3   Cronkhill, near Shrewsbury. By John Nash, c.1802. Photo. John Summerson, and plan from Summerson, *John Nash,* London, Allen & Unwin, 1935.

II 4   Design for "Four Cottages." From Joseph Gandy, *The Rural Architect,* 1805.

II 5   Design for "Italian Villa." From Robert Lugar, *Architectural Sketches,* 1805.

II 6   Design for "Double Cottage." Exterior and plan from Robert Lugar, *Architectural Sketches,* 1805.

II 7   Gwrych Castle, Denbighshire. By C. A. Busby and (?) Lloyd Bamford Hesketh, c.1814.

II 8   Design for "Italian Villa." From J. B. Papworth, *Rural Residences,* 1818.

II 9 Design for "Vicarage House." Elevation and plan from J. B. Papworth, *Rural Residences,* 1818.

II 10 Design for "Cottage Ornée." Perspective and plan from J. B. Papworth, *Rural Residences,* 1818.

II 11 Lodge, Villa Borghese, Rome. Perspective and plan from Charles Parker, *Villa rustica,* 1832.

II 12 Design for "Gothic Villa." By E. B. Lamb. From J. C. Loudon, *Encyclopedia of Cottage, Farm and Villa Architecture and Furniture,* 1833.

II 13 Design for "Gothic Villa." By E. B. Lamb. From *Architectural Magazine,* 1836.

II 14 Design for "Italian Villa." By E. B. Lamb. From *Architectural Magazine,* 1836.

II 15 Design for "Villa in the Cottage Style." From Francis Goodwin, *Domestic Architecture,* 1833.

II 16 Design for "Country Public House." By E. B. Lamb. From J. C. Loudon, *Encyclopedia of Cottage, Farm and Villa Architecture and Furniture,* 1833.

II 17 Royal Institution (now City Art Gallery), Mosley St., Manchester. By Sir Charles Barry, (1824) 1827–35.

II 18 St. Peter's Parish Church, Brighton. By Sir Charles Barry, (1823) 1824–28. Photo. N.B.R.

II 19 Travellers' Club House, Pall Mall, London. By Sir Charles Barry (1829) 1830–32. Garden front. Photo. N.B.R. Plan from W. H. Leeds, *The Travellers' Club House,* 1839.

II 20 Westminster New Palace, London. By Sir Charles Barry and A. N. W. Pugin, (1835–36) 1840–c.1865. Longitudinal section from *Building News,* 31 Dec. 1858.

II 21 Westminster New Palace, London. By Sir Charles Barry, A. N. W. Pugin and E. M. Barry, (1835–36) 1840–c.1865. Plan of principal floor from Alfred Barry, *Life and Works of Sir Charles Barry,* 1867.

II 22 Original design for Westminster New Palace, London. By Sir Charles Barry and A. N. W. Pugin, c.1836. South elevation from drawing at Royal Institute of British Architects.

II 23 Original design for Westminster New Palace, London. By Sir Charles Barry and A. N. W. Pugin, c.1836. North elevation from drawing at R.I.B.A.

II 24 Original design for Westminster New Palace, London. By Sir Charles Barry and A. N. W. Pugin, c.1836. West elevation from drawing at R.I.B.A.

II 25 Original design for Westminster New Palace. By Sir Charles Barry and A. N. W. Pugin. Perspective of river front, 1836. Photo. *Picture Post.*

II 26 King Edward's Free Grammar School, New St., Birmingham. By Sir Charles Barry, (1833) 1834–37. From Alfred Barry, *Life and Works of Sir Charles Barry,* 1867.

III 1   Church of Our Lady, Lisson Grove, London N.W.8. By J. J. Scoles, 1833–34. Photo. N.B.R.

III 2   "Contrasted Public Inns." From A. N. W. Pugin, *Contrasts*, 1836.

III 3   Design for a Norman church. From G. E. Hamilton, *Designs for Rural Churches*, 1836.

III 4   St. Augustine's, Tunbridge Wells. By Joseph Ireland, 1837–38.

III 5   St. Clement's, Oxford. Architect and date unknown. Photo. N.B.R.

III 6   St. Marie's, Bridgegate, Derby. By A. N. W. Pugin, 1838–39. West front. Photo. N.B.R.

III 7   St. Marie's, Bridgegate, Derby. By A. N. W. Pugin, 1838–39. Interior (painted decoration renewed 1930). Photo. N.B.R.

III 8   St. Marie's, Bridgegate, Derby. By A. N. W. Pugin, 1838–39. Plan, with indication of projected eastward extension, from A. N. W. Pugin, *The Present State of Ecclesiastical Architecture in England*, 1843.

III 9   St. Marie's, Bridgegate, Derby. By A. N. W. Pugin, 1838–39. Nave arcade and clerestorey. Photo. N.B.R.

III 10 The churches of A. N. W. Pugin. From A. N. W. Pugin, *Apology for the Revival of Christian Architecture in England*, 1843.

III 11 St. George's, Lambeth Rd., Southwark, London. By A. N. W. Pugin, 1840–48. Interior after blitz. Photo. N.B.R.

III 12 Project for St. George's, Southwark. By A. N. W. Pugin, 1838. Exterior from Benjamin Ferrey, *Recollections of A. N. Welby Pugin*, 1861.

III 13 St. George's, Lambeth Rd., Southwark, London. By A. N. W. Pugin, 1838. Plan from A. N. W. Pugin, *The Present State*, 1843.

III 14 Project for St. George's, Southwark. By A. N. W. Pugin, 1838. Interior from Benjamin Ferrey, *Recollections of A. N. Welby Pugin*, 1861.

III 15 Bishop Ryder's Church, Gem St., Birmingham. By Rickman and Hussey, 1837–38. Photo. N.B.R.

III 16 St. Chad's, Bath St., Birmingham. By A. N. W. Pugin, 1839–41. Exterior (with modern northwest chapel). Photo. N.B.R.

III 17 St. Chad's, Bath St., Birmingham. By A. N. W. Pugin, 1839–41. Interior. Photo. N.B.R.

III 18 St. Chad's, Bath St., Birmingham. By A. N. W. Pugin, 1839–41. West front. Photo. N.B.R.

III 19 St. Wilfrid's, Hulme, Manchester. By A. N. W. Pugin, 1839–42. Perspective and plan from A. N. W. Pugin, *The Present State*, 1843.

III 20 St. Oswald's, Old Swan, Liverpool. By A. N. W. Pugin, 1840–42. Perspective from southeast from A. N. W. Pugin, *The Present State*, 1843. West front, photo. J. R. Johnson.

III 21 "Contrasted Residences of the Poor." From A. N. W. Pugin, *Contrasts*, 2d ed. 1841.

III 22 "Contrasted English Towns, 1840 and 1440." From A. N. W. Pugin, *Contrasts*, 2d ed. 1841.

III 23 St. Mary's, Stockton-on-Tees, Co. Durham. By A. N. W. Pugin, 1840–42. From A. N. W. Pugin, *The Present State*, 1843.

III 24 An ideal medieval parish church. From A. N. W. Pugin, *True Principles of Christian or Pointed Architecture*, 1841.

III 25 Approved and disapproved moldings. From A. N. W. Pugin, *True Principles*, 1841.

III 26 St. Giles's, Cheadle, Staffordshire. By A. N. W. Pugin, 1841–46. Exterior from northeast. Photo. Marcus Whiffen. Plan from A. N. W. Pugin, *The Present State*, 1843.

III 27 St. Giles's, Cheadle, Staffordshire. By A. N. W. Pugin, 1841–46. Interior from *Illustrated London News*, 9 January 1847.

III 28 St. Giles's, Cheadle, Staffordshire. By A. N. W. Pugin, 1841–46. Interior showing chancel screen.

III 29 St. Barnabas's, Derby Rd., Nottingham. By A. N. W. Pugin, 1842–44. Projected chancel decorations from A. N. W. Pugin, *The Present State*, 1843.

III 30 St. Barnabas's, Derby Rd., Nottingham. By A. N. W. Pugin, 1842–44. Plan from A. N. W. Pugin, *The Present State*, 1843.

III 31 St. Barnabas's, Derby Rd., Nottingham. By A. N. W. Pugin, 1842–44. Nave looking east. Photo. N.B.R.

III 32 St. Barnabas's, Derby Rd., Nottingham. By A. N. W. Pugin, 1842–44. Exterior from northeast. Photo. N.B.R.

III 33 St. Barnabas's, Derby Rd., Nottingham. By A. N. W. Pugin, 1842–44. Exterior from south. Photo. N.B.R.

III 34 St. Augustine's, West Cliff, Ramsgate, Kent. By A. N. W. Pugin, 1846–51. Interior, looking east from south transept. Photo. N.B.R.

III 35 St. Augustine's, West Cliff, Ramsgate, Kent. By A. N. W. Pugin, 1846–51. Exterior from southeast. Photo. N.B.R.

III 36 St. Augustine's, West Cliff, Ramsgate, Kent. Floor tiles with Pugin's arms and monogram. Photo. N.B.R.

III 37 Church of Our Lady of Victories, Clapham Park Rd., London S.W.4. By W. W. Wardell, 1849–52. Photo. N.B.R.

III 38 St. John's, White Cross Bank, Salford. By Hadfield and Weightman, 1844–48. From Charles L. Eastlake, *History of the Gothic Revival*, 1872.

III 39 Church of the Immaculate Conception, Farm St., Grosvenor Square, London W 1. By J. J. Scoles, 1844–49. From *Builder*, 2 June 1849.

III 40 Church of the Holy Apostles, Clifton Rd., Bristol. Interior, 1847–49. Architect unknown. Photo. N.B.R.

III 41 St. Raphael's, Kingston-on-Thames, Surrey. By Charles Parker, 1846–47. From *Builder*, 18 Dec. 1847.

IV 1 Church of Holy Trinity, Blackheath Hill, London S.E.10. By J. W. Wild, 1838–39. From Companion to the *British Almanac*, 1840.

IV 2 St. Paul's, Valetta, Malta. Begun 1839. From *Illustrated London News*, 19 Jan. 1850.

IV 3   St. Laurence's, High St., Southampton. By J. W. Wild, 1839. From Companion to the *British Almanac*, 1840.

IV 4   St. Peter's Parish Church, Kirkgate, Leeds. By R. D. Chantrell, 1839–41. Exterior from northeast. Photo. Charles R. H. Pickard and Son.

IV 5   St. Peter's Parish Church, Kirkgate, Leeds. By R. D. Chantrell, 1839–41. Interior. Photo. N.B.R.

IV 6   Ss. Mary and Nicholas's, Wilton, Wiltshire. By Wyatt and Brandon, 1840–46. West front. Photo. N.B.R.

IV 7   Ss. Mary and Nicholas's, Wilton, Wiltshire. By Wyatt and Brandon, 1840–46. Plan from Companion to the *British Almanac*, 1843.

IV 8   Ss. Mary and Nicholas's, Wilton, Wiltshire. By Wyatt and Brandon, 1840–46. Interior from *Illustrated London News*, 4 Aug. 1849.

IV 9   Mill Hill Unitarian Chapel, Park Row, Leeds. By Bowman and Crowther, 1847–48. Photo. J. R. Johnson.

IV 10   Christ Church, Christchurch Rd., Streatham, London S.W.2. By J. W. Wild, 1840–42. Photo. J. R. Johnson.

IV 11   Great Thornton Street Chapel, Hull. By Lockwood and Allom, 1843. From *Illustrated London News*, 27 May 1843.

IV 12   Church at Scofton, Nottinghamshire. By Ambrose Poynter, c.1840. From Charles Anderson, *Ancient Models*, new ed. 1841.

IV 13   St. Matthew's, Otterbourne, Hampshire. By W. C. Yonge, c.1840. Photo. H. W. Salmon and Son.

IV 14   St. Jude's, Manningham, Bradford. By Walker Rawstone, 1841–43. Photo. J. R. Johnson.

IV 15   St. Jude's, Old Bethnal Green Rd., London E.2. By Henry Clutton, 1844–46. Interior after blitz. Photo. N.B.R.

IV 16   All Saints' Parish Church, Leamington, Warwickshire. By the Reverend John Craig, 1843–49. Photo. Walden Hammond.

IV 17   St. Saviour's, Cavalier Hill, Leeds. By J. M. Derick, 1842–45. Photo. N.B.R.

IV 18   Christ Church, Endell St., St. Giles's, London W.C.2. By Benjamin Ferrey, 1842–44. From *Builder*, 8 March 1845.

IV 19   St. Giles's, Camberwell Church St., London S.E.5. By Scott and Moffatt, 1842–44. Exterior from north. Photo. J. R. Johnson.

IV 20   St. Giles's, Camberwell Church St., London S.E.5. By Scott and Moffatt. Interior from *Illustrated London News*, 28 Dec. 1844.

IV 21   Memorial Church, Colabah, India. By J. M. Derick, c.1844. From *Illustrated London News*, 1 Feb. 1845.

IV 22   St. Stephen's, Lever Bridge, Bolton-le-Moors. By Edmund Sharpe, 1842–45. From *Illustrated London News*, 1 Feb. 1845.

IV 23   Church of Holy Trinity, Gloucester Terrace, Paddington, London, W.2. By Thomas Cundy II, 1844–46. Photo. N.B.R.

IV 24   Martyrs' Memorial, St. Giles St., Oxford. By Sir G. G. Scott, 1841.

IV 25   Church of Holy Trinity, Platt Lane, Rusholme, Manchester. By Edmund Sharpe, 1844–46. Photo. Palmer.

IV 26   St. Alkmund's, Bridgegate, Derby. By I. H. Stevens, 1844–46. Photo. N.B.R.

IV 27   St. Andrew's, Leeds. By Scott and Moffatt, 1844–45. Photo. N.B.R.

IV 28   St. Mark's, Swindon, Berkshire. By Scott and Moffatt, 1843–45. From *Illustrated London News*, 11 Oct. 1845.

IV 29   Walter Scott Monument, East Prince's St. Gardens, Edinburgh. By E. Meikle Kemp, (1836) 1840–46. Photo. F. C. Inglis.

V 1   Clapham Congregational Church, Grafton Sq., London S.W.4. By John Tarring, 1850–52. From *Builder*, 1852.

V 2   Cavendish Street Independent Chapel, Manchester. By Edward Walters, 1847–48. From *Illustrated London News*, 20 Mar. 1847.

V 3   Particular Baptist Chapel, Belvoir St., Leicester. By J. A. Hansom, 1844–45. From *Illustrated London News*, 25 Oct. 1845.

V 4   Central Baptist Chapel, Bloomsbury St., Holborn, London W.C.1. By John Gibson, 1845–48. Photo. N.B.R.

V 5   Accepted design for Nikolaikirche, Hamburg. By Sir G. G. Scott, (1844) 1845–63. From *Illustrated London News*, 9 Aug. 1845.

V 6   St. Andrew's, Wells St., Marylebone, London. By Dawkes and Hamilton, 1845–47 (re-erected in Church Lane, Kingsbury, Middlesex, 1933–34). From *Builder*, 2 Jan. 1847.

V 7   St. Matthew's, City Road, London N.1. By Sir G. G. Scott (with tower reputedly designed by G. E. Street), 1847–48. Photo. N.B.R.

V 8   Independent Church, Glasgow. By J. T. Emmett, 1852. From *Illustrated London News*, 19 June 1852.

V 9   St. Peter's, Tewksbury Rd., Cheltenham, Gloucestershire. By S. W. Dawkes, 1847–49. Exterior from southeast. Photo. N.B.R.

V 10   St. Peter's, Tewksbury Rd., Cheltenham, Gloucestershire. By S. W. Dawkes, 1847–49. Interior. Photo. N.B.R.

V 11   St. Ann's, New St., Alderney. By Sir G. G. Scott, 1847–50. From *Illustrated London News*, 5 Oct. 1850.

V 12   St. Matthias's, Chilton St., Bethnal Green, London E.2. By Wyatt and Brandon, 1847–48. Photo. J. R. Johnson.

V 13   St. Saviour's Vicarage, Coalpitheath, Gloucestershire. By William Butterfield, 1844–45. Photo. N.B.R.

V 14   Lychgate, St. Saviour's Churchyard, Coalpitheath, Gloucestershire. By William Butterfield, 1844–45. From Ecclesiological late Cambridge Camden Society, *Instrumenta ecclesiastica*, 1847.

V 15   Anglican Cathedral, St. John's, Newfoundland. By Sir G. G. Scott, begun 1846. From *Illustrated London News*, 23 June 1849.

V 16   Original design for St. Mary Magdalene's, Munster Sq., London N.W.1. By R. C. Carpenter, 1849. From *Ecclesiologist*, Vol. 10.

V 17   St. Mary Magdalene's, Munster Sq., London N.W.1. By R. C. Carpenter, 1849–52. Interior. Photo. J. R. Johnson.

V 18   St. Paul's, St. Paul St., Manningham, Bradford. By Mallinson and Healey, 1847–48. Photo. J. R. Johnson.

V 19   St. Thomas's, Southgate St., Winchester. By E. W. Elmslie, (1844) 1845–46 (tower completed 1856–57). Photo. H. W. Salmon and Son.

V 20   Design for Anglican Cathedral, Colombo, Ceylon. By R. C. Carpenter, 1847. Side elevation and section from *Civil Engineer and Architect's Journal*, 1 June 1861.

V 21   Original design for St. Paul's, West St., Brighton. By R. C. Carpenter, 1846. From *Ecclesiologist*, Vol. 5.

V 22   St. Paul's, West St., Brighton. By R. C. Carpenter, 1846–48. Interior. Photo. N.B.R.

V 23   St. Paul's, West St., Brighton. By R. C. Carpenter, 1846–48. East portal. Photo. N.B.R.

V 24   St. John's College, Hurstpierpoint, Sussex. By R. C. Carpenter, 1851–53. From *Illustrated London News*, 25 June 1853.

V 25   St. Stephen's, Rochester Row, Westminster, London S.W.1. By Benjamin Ferrey, 1847–50. Exterior. Photo. J. R. Johnson.

V 26   St. Stephen's, Rochester Row, Westminster, London S.W.1. By Benjamin Ferrey, 1847–50. Interior. Photo. J. R. Johnson.

V 27   St. Barnabas's, St. Barnabas St., Pimlico, London S.W.1. By Thomas Cundy II and (?) William Butterfield, 1846–50. Photo. J. R. Johnson.

V 28   St. Barnabas's Clergy House, Ranelagh Grove, Pimlico, London S.W.1. By Thomas Cundy II and (?) William Butterfield, 1847–48. Photo. J. R. Johnson.

V 29   St. Barnabas's, St. Barnabas St., Pimlico, London S.W.1. By Thomas Cundy II and (?) William Butterfield, 1846–50. Interior from *Illustrated London News*, 15 June 1850.

V 30   Church of Holy Trinity, Bessborough Gardens, Westminster, London S.W.1. By J. L. Pearson, 1849–52. Photo. J. R. Johnson.

V 31   Independent Chapel, Boston, Lincolnshire. By Stephen Lewin, 1849–50. From *Builder*, 9 Nov. 1850.

V 32   All Saints', Thirkleby, Yorkshire. By E. B. Lamb, 1848–50. From *Builder*, 12 Oct. 1850.

V 33   St. Thomas's, Coventry. By Sharpe and Paley, 1848–49. Exterior from northwest. Photo. N.B.R.

V 34   St. Thomas's, Coventry. By Sharpe and Paley, 1848–49. Interior. Photo. N.B.R.

V 35   Catholic Apostolic Church, Gordon Sq., Bloomsbury, London W.C.1. By Brandon and Ritchie, 1850–54. Exterior from north. Photo. N.B.R.

V 36   Catholic Apostolic Church, Gordon Sq., Bloomsbury, London W.C.1. Interior from *Builder*, 18 June 1859.

V 37   Caledonia Rd. Free Church, Glasgow. By Alexander Thomson, 1856–57. Photo. T. and R. Annan and Sons.

VI 1   Trentham Park, near Stoke-on-Trent. Italian gardens by Sir Charles Barry and W. A. Nesfield, c.1835–40. From *Illustrated London News*, 16 Oct. 1847.

VI 2   Trentham Park, near Stoke-on-Trent. As altered by Sir Charles Barry, c.1835–c.1850. Photo. *Country Life*.

VI 3   Town Hall, Crossley St., Halifax. By Sir Charles Barry and E. M. Barry, (1859)1860–62. From *Builder*, 21 Jan. 1860.

VI 4   Reform Club House, Pall Mall, London. By Sir Charles Barry, (1837) 1838–40. Elevation from *Surveyor, Engineer and Architect*, 1840.

VI 5   Reform Club House, Pall Mall, London. By Sir Charles Barry, (1837) 1838–40. Plan from *Civil Engineer and Architect's Journal*, Dec. 1840.

VI 6   Reform Club House, Pall Mall, London. By Sir Charles Barry, (1837) 1838–40. The north front, with the Travellers' Club House beyond. Photo. J. R. Johnson.

VI 7   Carlton Club House, Pall Mall, London. Winning project by Sydney Smirke for new front, 1846–47. From *Builder*, 8 May 1847.

VI 8   Conservative Club House, St. James's St., London. By George Basevi and Sydney Smirke, 1843–44. From *Illustrated London News*, 10 Feb. 1844.

VI 9   Army and Navy Club House, Pall Mall, London. By Parnell and Smith, 1848–51. From *Illustrated London News*, 1 Mar. 1851.

VI 10 Moxhay's Hall of Commerce, Threadneedle St., London, 1842–3. From *Illustrated London News*, 30 July 1843.

VI 11 Hall of Physicians, Queen St., Edinburgh. By Thomas Hamilton, 1844–45. From A. E. Richardson, *Monumental Classic Architecture in Great Britain and Ireland . . .* , London. B. T. Batsford [1914].

VI 12 Southampton Yacht Club, Southampton. By T. S. Hack, 1845. From *Illustrated London News*, 18 Sept. 1846.

VI 13 Mansion, Kensington Palace Gardens, London. By J. T. Knowles, 1847. Photo J. R. Johnson.

VI 14 Hudson Mansion, Albert Gate, Knightsbridge, London. By Thomas Cubitt, 1843–45. Photo. J. R. Johnson. (Conservatory not original.)

VI 15 Sheffield Athenaeum and Mechanics' Institute, Surrey and Tudor Sts., Sheffield. By George Alexander, 1847–48. From *Illustrated London News*, 4 Sept. 1847.

VI 16 Plymouth and Cottonian Libraries, Cornwall St., Plymouth. By George Wightwick, 1851–52. Front elevation from drawing at R.I.B.A.

VI 17 British Embassy, Constantinople. By Sir Charles Barry and W. J. Smith, (1842) 1845–47. From *Builder*, 27 Feb. 1848.

VI 18 Somerleyton Hall, near Lowestoft. As refaced by John Thomas, 1844–1851. From *Builder*, 7 June 1851.

VI 19   Highclere Castle, near Burghclere, Hampshire. As refaced by Sir Charles Barry, (1837) 1842–44. Photo. Marcus Whiffen.

VI 20   Bury Athenaeum, New Market St., Bury, Lancashire. By Sydney Smirke, 1850–51. From *Builder*, 9 Nov. 1850.

VI 21   Mansion, Kensington Palace Gardens, London. By R. R. Banks, 1843. From Companion to the *British Almanac*, 1846.

VI 22   Osborne House, near East Cowes, I. of W. By Prince Albert and Thomas Cubitt. Private pavilion, 1845–46. Photo. *Picture Post*.

VI 23   Osborne House, near East Cowes, I. of W. By Prince Albert and Thomas Cubitt. Garden front, 1847–49. Photo. *Picture Post*.

VI 24   Harlaxton Hall, near Grantham. By Anthony Salvin, 1834–c.1855. Photo. *Country Life*.

VII 1   City of London Prison, Camden Road, Holloway, London. By J. B. Bunning, 1851–52. From *Builder*, 14 June 1851.

VII 2   Pentonville Prison, Caledonian Rd., London. By Sir Charles Barry, 1841–42. Plan from *Builder*, 9 Oct. 1847.

VII 3   Pentonville Prison, Caledonian Rd., London. By Sir Charles Barry, 1841–42. Entrance block from *Illustrated London News*, 7 Jan. 1843.

VII 4   Berkshire County Gaol, Reading. By Scott and Moffatt, 1842–44. From *Illustrated London News*, 17 Feb. 1844.

VII 5   Dunrobin Castle, near Golspie, Sutherlandshire. By Sir Charles Barry and Leslie of Aberdeen, (1844) 1845–48. From *Illustrated London News*, 14 Sept. 1872.

VII 6   Board of Trade, Whitehall, London. By Sir Charles Barry, 1845–47. From *Illustrated London News*, 24 Oct. 1846.

VII 7   Bridgewater House, Cleveland Sq., London. By Sir Charles Barry, 1847–57. Entrance front. Photo. Helmut Gernsheim.

VII 8   Bridgewater House, Cleveland Sq., London. By Sir Charles Barry, 1847–57. Plan from *Builder*, 13 Oct. 1849.

VII 9   Bridgewater House, Cleveland Sq., London. By Sir Charles Barry, 1847–57. Ceiling in large drawing room. Photo. Helmut Gernsheim.

VII 10 Bridgewater House, Cleveland Sq., London. By Sir Charles Barry, 1847–57. Green Park front. Photo. Helmut Gernsheim.

VII 11 Bridgewater House, Cleveland Sq., London. By Sir Charles Barry, 1847–57. Doorcase in large drawing room. Photo. Helmut Gernsheim.

VII 12 Bridgewater House, Cleveland Sq., London. By Sir Charles Barry, 1847–57. Picture gallery after blitz. Photo. Helmut Gernsheim.

VII 13 Dorchester House, Park Lane, London. By Lewis Vulliamy, 1848–63. Park front. Photo. N.B.R.

VII 14 Dorchester House, Park Lane, London. By Lewis Vulliamy, 1848–63. Plan from drawing at R.I.B.A.

VII 15 Dorchester House, Park Lane, London. By Lewis Vulliamy, 1848–63. Entrance court. Photo. N.B.R.

VII 16 Great Western Hotel, Conduit St. East, Paddington, London. By

Philip C. Hardwick, 1851–53. From *Illustrated London News*, 18 Dec. 1852.

VII 17   Henry Thomas Hope House, Piccadilly at Down St., London. By P. C. Dusillon and T. L. Donaldson, 1848–51. Photo. N.B.R.

VII 18   Charles Russell House, 23 Park Lane, London. By W. B. Moffatt, 1846–48. Photo. N.B.R.

VII 19   General Hospital, Guinea St., Bristol. By W. B. Gingell, (1852) 1853–57. From *Building News*, 21 May 1858.

VII 20   Shrubland Park, near Ipswich. As remodeled by Sir Charles Barry, 1848–50. Photo. Marcus Whiffen.

VII 21   Cliveden, near Maidenhead. By Sir Charles Barry, 1849–51. Photo. *Country Life*.

VIII 1   St. Marie's Grange, near Salisbury. By A. N. W. Pugin, 1835–36. Plans and elevations from *Architectural Review*, Vol. 4.

VIII 2   Project for additions to Scarisbrick Hall, near Ormskirk, Lancashire. By A. N. W. Pugin, 1837. From Michael Trappes-Lomax, *Pugin, A Mediaeval Victorian*, London, Sheed & Ward, 1933.

VIII 3   Scarisbrick Hall, near Ormskirk, Lancashire. As remodeled by A. N. W. Pugin, 1837–52, and E. W. Pugin, 1860–68. From *Building News*, 24 Apr. 1868.

VIII 4   Scotney Castle, Lamberthurst, Kent. By Anthony Salvin, 1837–40. Photo. *Country Life*. Plan from drawing at R.I.B.A.

VIII 5   Alupka, Crimea near Yalta. By Edward Blore, 1837–40. From *Builder*, 27 July 1850.

VIII 6   Ramsey Abbey, Huntingdonshire. By Edward Blore, 1838–39. From drawing at R.I.B.A.

VIII 7   Worsley Hall, Eccles, near Manchester. By Edward Blore, (1839) 1840–45. Perspective and plan from *Builder*, 8 June 1850.

VIII 8   Wray Castle, Lake Windermere. By Horner of Liverpool, 1840–47.

VIII 9   Alton Castle, Staffordshire. As rebuilt by A. N. W. Pugin, c.1840. Photo. McCann.

VIII 10   St. Marie's Presbytery, Bridgegate, Derby. By A. N. W. Pugin, c.1840. Photo N.B.R.

VIII 11   Convent of the Sisters of Mercy, Hunter Rd., Birmingham. By A. N. W. Pugin, 1840–41. Photo N.B.R.

VIII 12   Alton Towers, Staffordshire. Exterior of hall by A. N. W. Pugin, 1849. Photo. Raphael Tuck and Sons.

VIII 13   Bilton Grange, near Rugby. By A. N. W. Pugin, 1841–46. From *Building News*, 29 May 1857.

VIII 14   The Grange, West Cliff, Ramsgate. By A. N. W. Pugin, 1841–43. Photo. N.B.R.

VIII 15   Tortworth Court, Cromhall, Gloucestershire. By S. S. Teulon. Perspective from *Builder*, 29 Oct. 1853. Plan from *Builder*, 19 Nov. 1853.

VIII 16 Enbrook, near Folkestone. By S. S. Teulon, 1853–55. Perspective from *Builder*, 16 Sept. 1854.

VIII 17 Enbrook, near Folkestone. By S. S. Teulon, 1853–55. Plan from *Builder*, 16 Sept. 1854.

VIII 18 Aldermaston Court, near Newbury. By P. C. Hardwick, 1848–51. Photo. *Country Life*.

VIII 19 Peckforton Castle, near Bunbury, Cheshire. By Anthony Salvin, 1846–50. *Corps de logis* from drawing at R.I.B.A.

VIII 20 Peckforton Castle, near Bunbury, Cheshire. By Anthony Salvin, 1846–50. Distant view from watercolor at R.I.B.A.

VIII 21 Peckforton Castle, near Bunbury, Cheshire. Anthony Salvin, 1846–50. View inside court from watercolor at R.I.B.A.

VIII 22 Lismore Castle, Waterford, Ireland. By Sir Joseph Paxton and G. H. Stokes, 1850–57. From *Building News*, 8 Jan. 1858.

VIII 23 Ruthin Castle, Ruthin, Denbigshire. By Henry Clutton, 1851–53. From *Builder*, 10 Sept. 1853.

VIII 24 Mentmore, near Cheddington, Buckinghamshire. By Sir Joseph Paxton and G. H. Stokes, 1852–54. From *Builder*, 10 Dec. 1857.

VIII 25 Balmoral Castle III, near Ballater, Fifeshire. By William Smith of Aberdeen and Prince Albert, 1853–55. Entrance front. Photo. *Picture Post*.

VIII 26 Balmoral Castle I, near Ballater, Fifeshire. By William Smith of Aberdeen, c.1845. From *Illustrated London News*, 1 Sept. 1849.

VIII 27 Balmoral Castle III, near Ballater, Fifeshire. By William Smith of Aberdeen and Prince Albert, 1853–55. Garden front. Photo. *Picture Post*.

VIII 28 Balmoral Castle III, near Ballater, Fifeshire. By William Smith of Aberdeen and Prince Albert, 1853–55. Distant view. Photo. *Picture Post*.

VIII 29 Buchanan House, near Glasgow. By William Burn, 1851–54. Perspective, dated 16 Jan. 1852, and plan, dated Mar. 1853, from drawings at R.I.B.A.

VIII 30 Project for Fonthill House, near Hinton, Wiltshire. By William Burn, c.1847. From watercolor at R.I.B.A.

VIII 31 Fonthill House, near Hinton, Wiltshire. By William Burn, c.1847–52. Photo. *Country Life*.

VIII 32 Clonghanadfoy Castle, near Limerick, Ireland. By G. F. Jones of York, c.1848–50. From *Builder*, 23 Nov. 1850.

VIII 33 Balentore, Scotland. By William Burn, c.1850. From watercolor at R.I.B.A.

VIII 34 Bylaugh Hall, near East Dereham, Norfolk. By Banks and Barry, 1849–52. From *Building News*, 26 Mar. 1869.

VIII 35 Grittleton House, near Chippenham, Wiltshire. By James Thomson, c.1845–60. From *Builder*, 30 Apr. 1853.

VIII 36   Vinters, near Maidstone. As remodeled by C. J. Richardson, 1850. From *Builder*, 5 Oct. 1850.

IX 1   Buckingham Palace, London. East front by Edward Blore, 1846–48.

IX 2   Buckingham Palace, London. East front by Edward Blore, 1846–48. Central Pavilion. From *Builder*, 28 Aug. 1847.

IX 3   Buckingham Palace, London. Chapel by Edward Blore, 1842–43. From *Illustrated London News*, 8 Apr. 1843.

IX 4   Buckingham Palace, London. Ballroom by Sir James Pennethorne, 1852–55. From *Builder*, 31 May 1856.

IX 5   Buckingham Palace, London. South wing by Sir James Pennethorne, 1852–55. From *Illustrated London News*, 1 Mar. 1856.

IX 6   Buckingham Palace, London. Supper Room by Sir James Pennethorne, 1852–55. From *Illustrated London News*, 18 July 1857.

IX 7   St. Stephen's Cloisters, Westminster New Palace, London. Built c.1526–29 but restored by Sir Charles Barry and A. N. W. Pugin. From *Builder*, 25 Oct. 1851.

IX 8   Westminster New Palace, London. By Sir Charles Barry and A. N. W. Pugin. House of Lords, 1840–46. Photo. Valentine and Sons.

IX 9   Westminster New Palace, London. By Sir Charles Barry and A. N. W. Pugin. Peers' Lobby, 1840–46. From *Illustrated London News*, 24 Apr. 1847.

IX 10   Westminster New Palace, London. By Sir Charles Barry and A. N. W. Pugin. Queen Victoria on throne in House of Lords receiving Speech from Lord Chancellor at Opening of Parliament. From *Illustrated London News*, 3 Feb. 1849.

IX 11   Westminster New Palace, London. By Sir Charles Barry and A. N. W. Pugin. Exterior of House of Lords, 1840–46. From *Illustrated London News*, 17 Apr. 1847.

IX 12   Westminster New Palace, London. By Sir Charles Barry and A. N. W. Pugin. Lower stages of Victoria Tower, 1840–52. From *Builder*, 13 Mar. 1858.

IX 13   Westminster New Palace, London. By Sir Charles Barry and A. N. W. Pugin. House of Commons, 1840–49, as first completed. From *Builder*, 5 Jan. 1850.

IX 14   Westminster New Palace, London. By Sir Charles Barry and A. N. W. Pugin. House of Commons as remodeled, 1850–51. From *Illustrated London News*, 7 Feb. 1852.

IX 15   Westminster New Palace, London. By Sir Charles Barry and A. N. W. Pugin. Victoria Lobby, 1840–46. From *Builder*, 26 June 1847.

IX 16   Westminster New Palace, London. By Sir Charles Barry and A. N. W. Pugin. Queen Victoria entering Royal Staircase on her way to open Parliament. From *Illustrated London News*, 7 Feb. 1852.

IX 17   Westminster New Palace, London. By Sir Charles Barry and A. N. W.

Pugin. Victoria Gallery with Queen Victoria approaching House of Lords. From *Illustrated London News*, 13 Nov. 1852.

IX 18 Westminster New Palace, London. By Sir Charles Barry and A. N. W. Pugin. Central Octagon. From *Illustrated London News*, 6 Nov. 1852. (Before installation of mosaics.)

IX 19 Westminster New Palace, London. By Sir Charles Barry and A. N. W. Pugin. St. Stephen's Hall. From *Illustrated London News*, 12 Feb. 1853.

IX 20 Westminster New Palace, London. By Sir Charles Barry and A. N. W. Pugin. St. Stephen's Porch and portion of west front. (Porch completed c.1853.) Photo. Valentine and Sons.

IX 21 Westminster Hall, London. 11th–13th centuries; enlarged by Henry Yevele and roofed by Hugh Herland, 1394–1402. St. Stephen's porch at end by Sir Charles Barry and A. N. W. Pugin. From *Illustrated London News*, 12 Feb. 1853.

IX 22 Westminster New Palace, London. By Sir Charles Barry and A. N. W. Pugin. Library of House of Lords as completed c.1852. Photo. Valentine and Sons.

IX 23 Westminster New Palace, London. By Sir Charles Barry and A. N. W. Pugin. Roofs seen from Victoria Tower with lantern over Central Octagon in foreground and Clock Tower to rear. From *Illustrated London News*, 28 Jan. 1860.

IX 24 Westminster New Palace, London. Top of Victoria Tower as projected by Sir Charles Barry before his death. From *Builder*, 27 Mar. 1858.

IX 25 Westminster New Palace, London. By Sir Charles Barry and A. N. W. Pugin. Belfry of Clock Tower in construction. From *Illustrated London News*, 5 Dec. 1857.

IX 26 Museum of Economic Geology, London. By Sir James Pennethorne, (c.1845) 1847–48 (1851). Jermyn St. entrance. Photo. N.B.R.

IX 27 Museum of Economic Geology, London. By Sir James Pennethorne, (c.1845), 1847–48 (1851). Piccadilly front from *Illustrated London News*, 8 Apr. 1848.

IX 28 Museum of Economic Geology, London. By Sir James Pennethorne, (c.1845) 1847–48 (1851). Details of iron roof construction from *Builder*, 18 Nov. 1848.

IX 29 Museum of Economic Geology, London. By Sir James Pennethorne, (c.1845), 1847–48 (1851). Interior of gallery from *Builder*, 28 Oct. 1848.

IX 30 Record Office, Chancery Lane, London. By Sir James Pennethorne, (c.1847) 1851–70. The north front as originally projected from *Builder*, 11 Oct. 1851.

IX 31 Ordnance Office, London. By Sir James Pennethorne, 1850–51. Pall Mall front from *Builder*, 16 Aug. 1851.

IX 32 General Post Office, St. Martin-le-Grand, London. Sorting Room added by Sydney Smirke, 1845. From *Builder*, 24 Jan. 1846.

X 1   The Royal Exchange, London. By Sir William Tite, (1839) 1840–44. West front from *Architect, Engineer and Surveyor*, 1840.

X 2   The Royal Exchange, London. By Sir William Tite, (1839) 1841–44. South front from *Illustrated London News*, 26 Oct. 1844.

X 3   The Royal Exchange, London. By Sir William Tite, (1839) 1841–44. Court, with Royal procession at opening, from *Illustrated London News*, 2 Nov. 1844.

X 4   The Royal Exchange, London. By Sir William Tite, (1839) 1841–44. South and east fronts from *Illustrated London News*, 26 Oct. 1844.

X 5   Fitzwilliam Museum, Trumpington St., Cambridge. By George Basevi and C. R. Cockerell, 1837–47. Photo. *Picture Post*.

X 6   St. George's Hall, Lime St., Liverpool. By H. L. Elmes, Sir Robert Rawlinson, and C. R. Cockerell, (1839–40) 1841–47, 1847–49, 1851–54 (1856). East front. Photo. *Picture Post*.

X 7   St. George's Hall, Lime St., Liverpool. By H. L. Elmes, Robert Rawlinson, and C. R. Cockerell, (1839–40) 1841–47, 1847–49, 1851–54 (1856). Plan from *Builder*, 6 Jan. 1855.

X 8   St. George's Hall, Lime St., Liverpool. By H. L. Elmes, Robert Rawlinson, and C. R. Cockerell, (1839–40) 1841–47, 1847–49, 1851–54 (1856). North end. Photo. N.B.R.

X 9   University Galleries and Taylor Institute (Ashmolean), Beaumont and St. Giles Sts., Oxford. By C. R. Cockerell, (1840) 1841–45. Elevation toward Beaumont St. from *Builder*, 24 Oct. 1846.

X 10   University Galleries and Taylor Institute (Ashmolean), Beaumont and St. Giles Sts., Oxford. By C. R. Cockerell, (1840) 1841–45. Plan from *Builder*, 24 Oct. 1846.

X 11   University Galleries and Taylor Institute (Ashmolean), Beaumont and St. Giles Sts., Oxford. By C. R. Cockerell, (1840) 1841–45. East front from A. E. Richardson, *Monumental Classic Architecture* [1914].

X 12   Hall and Library of Lincoln's Inn, London. By Philip and P. C. Hardwick, 1843–45. West front toward Lincoln's Inn Fields from *Illustrated London News*, 1 Nov. 1845.

X 13   Hall and Library of Lincoln's Inn, London. By Philip and P. C. Hardwick, 1843–45. Plan from *Illustrated London News*, 1 Nov. 1845.

X 14   Coal Exchange, Lower Thames St., London. By J. B. Bunning, 1846–49. Court from *Builder*, 29 Sept. 1849.

X 15   Coal Exchange, Lower Thames St., London. By J. B. Bunning, 1846–49. From southeast. Photo. N.B.R.

X 16   Coal Exchange, Lower Thames St., London. By J. B. Bunning, 1846–49. Perspective from drawing at R.I.B.A.

X 17   Coal Exchange, Lower Thames St., London. By J. B. Bunning, 1846–49. Dome panels of tree-ferns designed by Melhado and executed by Sang. Photo. Helmut Gernsheim.

X 18 Coal Exchange, Lower Thames St., London. By J. B. Bunning, 1846–49. Colliery in panel painted by Sang. Photo. Helmut Gernsheim.

X 19 Coal Exchange, Lower Thames St., London. By J. B. Bunning, 1846–49. Plan from *Allgemeine Bauzeitung* (Vienna), 1850.

X 20 Coal Exchange, Lower Thames St., London. By J. B. Bunning, 1846–49. "Jolly Miner" in panel painted by Sang. Photo. Helmut Gernsheim.

X 21 Coal Exchange, Lower Thames St., London. By J. B. Bunning, 1846–49. Dome ribs. Photo. Helmut Gernsheim.

X 22 Coal Exchange, Lower Thames St., London. By J. B. Bunning, 1846–49. Second-storey stanchions. Photo. Helmut Gernsheim.

X 23 Coal Exchange, Lower Thames St., London. By J. B. Bunning, 1846–49. Ground-storey stanchions. Photo. Helmut Gernsheim.

X 24 Coal Exchange, Lower Thames St., London. By J. B. Bunning, 1846–49. First-storey stanchions. Photo. Helmut Gernsheim.

X 25 Metropolitan Cattle Market (Caledonian Market), Copenhagen Fields, London. By J. B. Bunning, 1850–54. Birdseye view from *Illustrated London News*, 2 Dec. 1854.

X 26 Clock Tower and Offices, Caledonian Market, London. By J. B. Bunning, 1850–54. Elevation from *Building News*, 1855, p. 921.

X 27 White Horse Tavern, Caledonian Market, London. By J. B. Bunning, 1850–54. Photo. J. R. Johnson.

X 28 Billingsgate Market, Lower Thames St., London. By J. B. Bunning, 1850–52. From *Builder*, 3 Jan. 1852.

X 29 Corn Exchange, Grass Market, Edinburgh. By David Cousin, 1847–49. Front from *Builder*, 17 June 1848. Interior from *Illustrated London News*, 8 Dec. 1849.

X 30 Town Hall and Market, Truro, Cornwall. By Christopher Eales, 1845–46. Front and rear. Photos. N.B.R.

X 31 Custom House, Ipswich. By J. M. Clark, 1843–45. From *Illustrated London News*, 26 July 1845.

X 32 St. Martin's Hall, Long Acre, London. By William Westmacott, 1847–50. From *Illustrated London News*, 26 June 1847.

X 33 Royal Academy Gold Medal project for a "Wellington College." By R. N. Shaw, 1853. From *Illustrated London News*, 31 Dec. 1853.

X 34 Wellington College, Sandhurst, Berkshire. Original design by John Shaw II, 1855. From *Builder*, 16 Feb. 1856.

X 35 Kneller Hall Training School, Whitton, Middlesex. By George Mair, 1848–50. From *Illustrated London News*, 23 Feb. 1850.

X 36 St. George's Hall, Bradford. By Lockwood and Mawson, 1851–53. Side and rear. Photos. N.B.R.

X 37 St. George's Hall, Lime St., Liverpool. By H. L. Elmes, Robert Rawlinson, and C. R. Cockerell, (1839–40) 1841–47, 1847–49, 1851–54. Opening of Great Hall from *Illustrated London News*, 23 Sept. 1854.

X 38 Concert Room, St. George's Hall, Lime St., Liverpool. By H. L. Elmes and C. R. Cockerell, (1839–40) 1851–56. Photo. N.B.R.

X 39 Concert Room, St. George's Hall, Lime St., Liverpool. By H. L. Elmes and C. R. Cockerell, (1839–40) 1851–56. Stage. Photo. N.B.R.

X 40 National Gallery of Scotland, The Mound, Edinburgh. By W. H. Playfair, 1850–54. (With the Royal Scottish Institution, 1822–36, on the right, and the Free Church College, 1846–50, behind; both also by Playfair.) Photo. F. C. Inglis.

X 41 Royal Institution, Great Thornton St., Hull. By Cuthbert Brodrick, 1852–54. Detail of entrance doorway. Photo. N.B.R.

XI 1 Bank Chambers, 3 Cook St., Liverpool. By C. R. Cockerell, 1849–50. Photo. J. R. Johnson.

XI 2 London and Westminster Bank, Lothbury, London. By C. R. Cockerell, 1837–38. Original façade from Companion to the British Almanac, 1839.

XI 3 Legal and General Life Assurance Office, 10 Fleet St., London. By Thomas Hopper, c.1838. (On the right; building on the left by George Aitchison I, c.1855.) From Illustrated London News, 4 Apr. 1857.

XI 4 Sun Fire and Life Assurance Offices, Bartholomew Lane and Threadneedle St., London. By C. R. Cockerell, (1839) 1840–42. From A. E. Richardson, Monumental Classic Architecture [1914].

XI 5 Liverpool and London Insurance Offices, Dale St. and Exchange Pl., Liverpool. By C. R. Cockerell, 1856–58. Photo. N.B.R.

XI 6 Savings Bank, Bath. By George Alexander, 1840–41. From lithograph at R.I.B.A.

XI 7 Commercial Bank of Scotland, George St., Edinburgh. By David Rhind, 1844–46. Photo. F. C. Inglis.

XI 8 National Bank, Glasgow. By John Gibson, 1847–49. From Illustrated London News, 7 July 1849.

XI 9 Branch Bank of England, Castle and Cook Sts., Liverpool. By C. R. Cockerell, 1845–58. From A. E. Richardson, Monumental Classic Architecture [1914]. Front and side. Photo. N.B.R.

XI 10 Branch Bank of England, Broad St., Bristol. By C. R. Cockerell, 1844–46. Photo. N.B.R.

XI 11 Stanley Dock, Liverpool. By Jesse Hartley, 1852–56. Warehouses after blitz. Photo. J. R. Johnson.

XI 12 Royal Insurance Buildings, Dale and North John Sts., Liverpool. By William Grellier, 1846–49. From Builder, 23 Dec. 1848.

XI 13 Stanley Dock, Liverpool. By Jesse Hartley, 1852–56. Walls and entrances. Photo. J. R. Johnson.

XI 14 Imperial Assurance Office, Broad and Threadneedle Sts., London. By John Gibson, 1846–48. From Illustrated London News, 17 Mar. 1849.

XI 15 Queen's Assurance and Commercial Chambers, 42–44 Gresham St., corner King St. By Sancton Wood, 1851–52. Photo. J. R. Johnson.

XI 16 Sir Benjamin Heywood's (now Williams Deacon's) Bank, St. Ann's Sq.,

Manchester. By J. E. Gregan, 1848–49. St. Ann's St. elevation from *Builder*, 13 Jan. 1849. Entrance. Photo. N.B.R.

XI 17   Corn Exchange (left) and Bank, now Royal Insurance Office (right), Market Sq., Northampton. By Alexander and Hall, (1849) 1850–51, and E. F. Law, 1850, respectively. From *Illustrated London News*, 29 Mar. 1851.

XI 18   London and Westminster Bank, Bloomsbury Branch, Holborn, London. By Henry Baker, 1853–54. Elevation and plan from *Builder*, 18 June 1853.

XII 1   Brunswick Buildings, Brunswick and Fenwick Sts., Liverpool. By A. and G. Williams, 1841–42. From Companion to the *British Almanac*, 1843.

XII 2   Royal Exchange Buildings, Freeman's Pl., London. By Edward I'Anson and Son, 1844–45. From *Illustrated London News*, 4 Oct. 1845.

XII 3   Chambers, Staple Inn, Holborn, London. By Wigg and Pownall, 1842–43. From *Illustrated London News*, 27 May 1843.

XII 4   Nos. 93–105 New Oxford St., London. Possibly by Sir James Pennethorne, c. 1845–47. Photo. N.B.R.

XII 5   Faringdon St. North, London. As intended to be completed, 1843. From *Illustrated London News*, 24 Feb. 1844.

XII 6   Block of shops, New Coventry St., London. By Charles Mayhew, 1843–44. From *Illustrated London News*, 18 Oct. 1845.

XII 7   Nos. 44–50 New Oxford St., London. c.1845–47. Photo. N.B.R.

XII 8   Nos. 75–77 New Oxford St., London. Possibly by Sir James Pennethorne, c.1845–47. Photo. N.B.R.

XII 9   Terrace of shops and houses, Queen St., Glasgow. By James Wylson, 1848. From *Builder*, 15 July 1848.

XII 10   Colonial Buildings, Horse Fair and Windmill St., Birmingham, c.1845. Photo. N.B.R.

XII 11   Nos. 5–9 Aldermanbury, London. c.1840? Photo. N.B.R.

XII 12   Boote Buildings, Elliott St., Liverpool. 1846. Photo. J. R. Johnson.

XII 13   No. 50 Watling St., London. c.1843? Photo. J. R. Johnson.

XII 14   S. Schwabe Warehouse, 46–54 Mosley St., Manchester. By Edward Walters, 1845. Photo. J. R. Johnson.

XII 15   The Quadrant, Regent St., London. By John Nash, 1819–20, as revised by Sir James Pennethorne, 1848. From *Illustrated London News*, 4 Nov. 1848.

XII 16   James Brown, Son, and Co. Warehouse, 9 Portland St., Manchester. By Edward Walters, 1851–52. From *Illustrated London News*, 14 May 1853.

XII 17   Two shops in Market St., Manchester. By Starkey and Cuffley, 1851. Elevation from *Builder*, 31 May 1851.

XII 18   Warehouse, Portland and Parker Sts., Manchester. By J. E. Gregan, 1850. Elevation and plan from *Builder*, 31 Aug. 1850.

XII 19 Shops and houses, New Oxford St., London. By Henry Stansby, 1846. Elevation from Companion to the *British Almanac,* 1847.

XII 20 Warehouse in Mosley St., Manchester. Before 1851. From *Illustrated London News,* 25 Oct. 1851.

XII 21 Northern Schools, St. Martin's-in-the-Fields, Castle St., Long Acre, London. By J. W. Wild, 1849–50. Elevation from *Builder,* 22 Sept. 1849.

XII 22 Mr. Fair's Shop and House, Prince's St., Hanover Sq., London, 1842. From *Builder,* 15 Apr. 1843.

XII 23 Project for Grocer's Shop. By A. N. W. Pugin. From his *Apology for the Revival,* 1843.

XII 24 Perfumery shopfront, Piccadilly, London, 1850. From *Builder,* 12 Apr. 1851.

XII 25 Prefabricated shops and dwellings, Melbourne, Australia. Made by Samuel Hemming in Bristol, 1853. From *Builder,* 8 Apr. 1854.

XII 26 L. T. Piver shopfront, 160 Regent St., London. By Cambon, 1846. From *Illustrated London News,* 22 Aug. 1846.

XII 27 Shops in New Oxford St., London, 1851. From Companion to the *British Almanac,* 1851.

XII 28 Warehouse, 12 Temple St., Bristol. Perhaps by W. B. Gingell, c.1855. Photo. Victor Turl.

XII 29 W. H. Smith Building, 188–192 Strand, London. By H. R. Abraham, 1852. From *Illustrated London News,* 12 Mar. 1853.

XIII 1 Gloucester Sq., from Hyde Park Sq., Bayswater, London. 1837–c.1847. Northwest side being demolished in 1936. Photo. John Summerson.

XIII 2 Milner Sq., Islington, London. By Gough and Roumieu, 1841–43. Photo. *Country Life.*

XIII 3 Lonsdale Sq., Islington, London. By R. C. Carpenter, begun 1838. Photo. *Country Life.*

XIII 4 Royal Promenade, Victoria Sq., Clifton, Bristol. Begun 1837. Photo. N.B.R.

XIII 5 Worcester Terrace, Clifton, Bristol. Completed 1851–53 presumably from much earlier design. Photo. N.B.R.

XIII 6 Gloucester Sq., Bayswater, London. Southeast side, c.1840–45. Photo. N.B.R.

XIII 7 Lansdowne Place, Citadel Rd., Plymouth. Probably by George Wightwick, c.1845. Photo. N.B.R.

XIII 8 Nos. 4–8 Eastgate St., Winchester. c.1840. Photo. J. R. Johnson.

XIII 9 Nos. 10–20 Eastgate St., Winchester. c.1840. Photo J. R. Johnson.

XIII 10 Peacock Terrace, Liverpool Grove, Walworth, London, 1842. Photo. J. R. Johnson.

XIII 11 "Grecian Villa." By S. H. Brooks, 1839. From his *Designs for Cottage and Villa Architecture,* n.d.

XIII 12 Semidetached "second-rate" houses. From T. L. Walker, *Architectural Precedents,* 3rd ed., 1841.

XIII 13   "Villa in the Florentine Style." By Richard Brown. From his *Domestic Architecture*, 1842.

XIII 14   National School for 500 children. By Charles Parker. From his *Villa rustica*, Book Three, 1841.

XIII 15   "Villa in the Italian Style." By John White. From his *Rural Architecture*, Glasgow, 1845.

XIII 16   Jacobethan entrance. By John White. From his *Rural Architecture*, Glasgow, 1845.

XIII 17   £200 row houses. By Samuel Hemming, c.1855. Elevation and plan from his *Designs for Villas, Parsonages and other Houses*, n.d.

XIII 18   £670 parsonage house. By Samuel Hemming, c.1855. Elevation and plan from his *Designs for Villas*, n.d.

XIII 19   Semidetached £750 houses. By Samuel Hemming, c.1855. Elevation from his *Designs for Villas*, n.d.

XIII 20   Terrace in Lowndes Sq., Belgravia, London. By Lewis Cubitt, 1841–43. Elevation and plans of corner house from *Architect, Engineer and Surveyor*, 1841.

XIII 21   Lyppiat Terrace, Lyppiat Rd., Cheltenham. Probably by R. W. Jearrad, c.1845. Photo. N.B.R.

XIII 22   £1550 villa. By Samuel Hemming, c.1855. Elevation and plan from his *Designs for Villas*, etc., n.d.

XIII 23   Terrace with corner house, Westbourne Terrace, Paddington, London. Probably by R. P. Browne, c.1845. From lithograph at R.I.B.A.

XIII 24   Westbourne Terrace, Paddington, London, c.1845. Photo. Drake and Lasdun.

XIII 25   Quasi-semidetached houses, Westbourne Terrace, Paddington, London. Probably by R. P. Browne, c.1845–50. Photo. N.B.R.

XIII 26   Gloucester Crescent, Camden Town, London, c.1850. Photo. J. R. Johnson.

XIII 27   Kensington Gate, Gloucester Rd., South Kensington, London. Probably by Bean, c.1850. Photo. J. R. Johnson.

XIII 28   Quasi-semidetached houses, Gloucester Terrace, Paddington, London, c.1845–50. Photo. N.B.R.

XIII 29   College Terrace, Stepney, London, c.1845–50. Photo. N.B.R.

XIII 30   Llandudno, North Wales. By Wehnert and Ashdown (and others), 1849–55. From *Illustrated London News*, 15 Sept. 1855.

XIII 31   St. Ann's Villas, Norland Rd., London, c.1847. Photo. J. R. Johnson.

XIII 32   West London in the mid-50's. From *Wyld's New Plan of London for 1858*, London, Jas. Wyld, 1858.

XIII 33   Blenheim Mount, Manningham Lane, Bradford, c.1855. Photo. J. R. Johnson.

XIII 34   Terrace with shops below, St. George's Pl., Knightsbridge, London. By F. R. Beeston, c.1848. Elevation from Peter Nicholson, *Carpentry*, 1849.

XIII 35 Plan of Birkenhead, with proposed docks, published by James Law, 1844. Courtesy of Town Clerk, Birkenhead.

XIII 36 Plan of Birkenhead Park, Birkenhead. By Sir Joseph Paxton, 1842–44. From A. A. Ernouf and A. Alphand, *L'Art des Jardins,* 3rd ed., 1880, p. 217.

XIII 37 Semidetached houses, 39–41 White Ladies Road, Clifton, Bristol, c.1855. Photo. Victor Turl.

XIII 38 Birkenhead Park Lodge, 88 Park Rd. South, Birkenhead. By Lewis Hornblower, 1844. Photo. J. R. Johnson.

XIV 1 Gloucester Arms public house and contiguous houses, Gloucester Terrace, Paddington, London. c.1852. Photo. N.B.R.

XIV 2 Salt Mill, Saltaire, near Bradford, Yorkshire. By Lockwood and Mawson, and Sir William Fairbairn, 1851–53. From *Builder,* 19 Aug. 1854.

XIV 3 Salt Mill, Saltaire, near Bradford, Yorkshire. By Lockwood and Mawson, and Sir William Fairbairn, 1851–53. Entrance to offices.

XIV 4 Model Lodging House for Single Men, George St., St. Giles, London. By Henry Roberts, 1846–47. From *Illustrated London News,* 23 Jan. 1847.

XIV 5 Model Lodging Houses, Clerkenwell, London. By Henry Roberts, 1845–46. Perspective and plans from *Illustrated London News,* 11 Apr. 1846.

XIV 6 Model Houses for Families (flatted), Streatham and George Sts., Bloomsbury, London. By Henry Roberts, 1849–50. Exterior. Photo. N.B.R.

XIV 7 Model Houses for Families (flatted), Streatham and George Sts., Bloomsbury, London. By Henry Roberts, 1849–50. Access galleries in court. Photo. N.B.R.

XIV 8 Model Houses for Families (flatted), Streatham and George Sts., Bloomsbury, London. By Henry Roberts, 1849–50. Plan of ground floor from *Builder,* 14 July 1849.

XIV 9 Workmen's Dwellings (flatted), Birkenhead, 1845–47. From Companion to the *British Almanac,* 1848.

XIV 10 Project for Model Town Houses for the Middle Classes (flatted). By William Young, 1849. Perspective and plans from *Builder,* 1 Dec. 1849.

XIV 11 Apartment Houses in Victoria St. between Carlisle Pl. and Howick Pl., London. By Henry Ashton, 1852–54. General view looking east from *Illustrated London News,* 18 Nov. 1854.

XIV 12 Apartment Houses in Victoria St., London. By Henry Ashton, 1852–54. Typical upper-floor plan of one "house," with two apartments opening on one stair, from *Builder,* 3 Dec. 1853.

XIV 13 Terrace on south side of Woodhouse Sq., Leeds, c.1850–55. Photo. J. R. Johnson.

XIV 14 Prince Albert's Model Houses, Hyde Park, London (now in Kenning-

ton Park). By Henry Roberts, 1850–51. From *Illustrated London News*, 14 June 1851.

XIV 15 Prince's Terrace (now Prince's Gate), Kensington Rd., London. By Johnston, 1850–51. Front and rear elevations from *Architect, Surveyor and Engineer*, 26 July 1851.

XIV 16 Nos. 70–74 Eastgate St., Winchester, c.1850. Photo. J. R. Johnson.

XIV 17 St. Aidan's Terrace, Forest Rd., Birkenhead. Possibly by T. H. Wyatt, c.1853. Photo. J. R. Johnson.

XIV 18 South side of Grosvenor Sq., London. Three houses have Early Victorian fronts, all probably by Thomas Cundy II, c.1855. Photo. N.B.R.

XIV 19 Terrace in Hyde Park Sq., Bayswater, London, c.1840. Photo. N.B.R.

XIV 20 Terrace between Cleveland Sq. and Cleveland Gardens, Paddington, London, c.1850–55. Entrance front. Photo. N.B.R.

XIV 21 Terrace, Moray Pl., Strathbungo, Glasgow. By Alexander Thomson, 1860. Photo. T. and R. Annan and Sons.

XIV 22 Terrace between Cleveland Sq. and Cleveland Gardens, Paddington, London, c.1850–55. Garden front. Photo. N.B.R.

XIV 23 Terrace in Victoria Sq., Clifton, Bristol, c.1855. Photo. J. R. Johnson.

XIV 24 Walmer Crescent, Paisley Rd., Glasgow. By Alexander Thomson, 1858. Photo. G. C. Law.

XIV 25 Queen's Park Terrace (flatted), Eglinton St., Glasgow. By Alexander Thomson, 1859. Photo. T. and R. Annan and Sons.

XV 1 Liverpool and Manchester Railway Station, Liverpool (Lime St. I). By John Cunningham, opened in 1836. Shed from C. F. D. Marshall, *Centenary History of the Liverpool and Manchester Railway*, London, Locomotive Publishing Co., 1930.

XV 2 North-Western Railway Station, Liverpool (Lime St. II). Shed by Richard Turner, 1849–51. Part plan and section from *Civil Engineer and Architect's Journal*, 15 Mar. 1851.

XV 3 Liverpool and Manchester Railway Station, Liverpool (Lime St. I). Entrance screen by John Foster, completed 1836. From C. F. D. Marshall, *Centenary History of the Liverpool and Manchester Railway*, London, Locomotive Publishing Co., 1930.

XV 4 North-Western Railway Station, Liverpool (Lime St. II). Station block facing Lord Nelson St. By Sir William Tite, 1846–50. Elevation from *Builder*, 17 Feb. 1849.

XV 5 London and North-Western Railway Station, Liverpool (Lime St. II). By Sir William Tite, 1846–50. Plan from *Builder*, 17 Feb. 1849.

XV 6 London and Birmingham Railway Station, Euston Grove, London (Euston I). The "Arch" by Philip Hardwick, 1836–37. From J. C. Bourne, *Drawings of the London and Birmingham Railway*, 1839.

XV 7 London and Birmingham Station, Euston Grove, London (Euston I). By Robert Stephenson and Philip Hardwick, 1835–39. Plan from S. C. Brees, *Fourth Series of Railway Practice*, 1847.

XV 8   London and Birmingham Station, Euston Grove, London (Euston I). Original departure and arrival sheds by Robert Stephenson, 1835–39. From J. C. Bourne, *Drawings of the London and Birmingham Railway*, 1839.

XV 9   Projects for railway bridges on the "Antient Principles," with stations. By A. N. W. Pugin. From his *Apology for the Revival*, 1843.

XV 10   London and Southampton Railway Station (now Transport Museum), Nine Elms Rd., Vauxhall, London (Nine Elms). By Joseph Locke and Sir William Tite, 1837–38. Photo. N.B.R.

XV 11   Trijunct Railway Station and North Midland Station Hotel, Derby. By Francis Thompson and Robert Stephenson, 1839–41. From lithograph by S. Russell.

XV 12   Trijunct Railway Station, Derby. By Robert Stephenson and Francis Thompson, 1839–41. Sheds from lithograph by S. Russell.

XV 13   Railway station, Wingfield, Derbyshire. By Francis Thompson, c.1840. Elevation, "revised to serve as a cottage residence," from J. C. Loudon, *Encyclopedia of Cottage, Farm and Villa Architecture and Furniture*, new ed., 1842.

XV 14   Railway station, Ambergate, Derbyshire. By Francis Thompson, c.1840. Elevation, "revised to serve as a cottage residence," from J. C. Loudon, *Encyclopedia of Cottage, Farm and Villa Architecture and Furniture*, new ed., 1842.

XV 15   Great Western Railway Station, under Bishop's Rd., Paddington, London (Paddington I). By I. K. Brunel, 1838. From J. C. Bourne, *History and Description of the Great Western Railway*, 1846.

XV 16   Great Western Railway Station, London (Paddington I). By I. K. Brunel, 1838. Section of shed from drawing at Chief Engineer's Office, Paddington.

XV 17   Clifton Suspension Bridge, Clifton Gorge, near Bristol. Designed and begun by I. K. Brunel, finished by W. H. Barlow, (1829) 1837–63. Photo. Garratt.

XV 18   Queen's Hotel, Cheltenham. By R. W. Jearrad, opened in 1837. Photo. A. R. Jay.

XV 19   Great Western (now Hydro) Hotel, Hotwells Rd., Bristol. By R. S. Pope, opened in 1839. Photo. J. R. Johnson.

XV 20   Great Western Station, Bristol (Temple Mead I). By I. K. Brunel, 1839–40. Plan, sections and elevations from S. C. Brees, *Fourth Series of Railway Practice*, 1847.

XV 21   Great Western Station, Bristol (Temple Mead I). By I. K. Brunel, 1839–40. Shed from J. C. Bourne, *History and Description of the Great Western Railway*, 1846.

XV 22   Great Northern Railway Station, Tanner Row, York. By T. G. Andrews, 1840–42. The triple shed, with the Queen entraining, from *Illustrated London News*, 6 Oct. 1849.

XV 23   Great Northern Station, Tanner Row, York. By T. G. Andrews, 1840–42. Departure-side elevation, with added storey for hotel accommodation indicated over head-block to right, from drawing at Engineer's Office in station.

XV 24   South-Eastern Railway Station, Southwark, London (Bricklayers' Arms). By Lewis Cubitt, 1842–44. Entrance screen from *Illustrated London News*, 4 May 1845.

XV 25   South-Eastern Railway Station, Southwark, London (Bricklayers' Arms). By Lewis Cubitt, 1842–44. Plan from *Civil Engineer and Architect's Journal*, Apr. 1844.

XV 26   Eastern Counties Railway Station, Cambridge. By Sancton Wood, 1844–45. From *Illustrated London News*, 2 Aug. 1845.

XV 27   Congleton Viaduct, North Staffordshire Railway. By J. C. Forsyth, opened 1849. From *Illustrated London News*, 16 June 1849.

XV 28   Croydon and Epsom Atmospheric Railway Station, Epsom. By J. R. and J. A. Brandon, 1844–45. From *Illustrated London News*, 1 Mar. 1845.

XV 29   Great Conservatory, Chatsworth, Derbyshire. By Sir Joseph Paxton and Decimus Burton, (1836) 1837–40. Photo. *Country Life.*

XV 30   King Eyambo's Palace, Calabar River, Africa. Prefabricated by John Walker in London, 1843–44. From *Builder*, 13 May 1843.

XV 31   Palm Stove, Royal Botanic Gardens, Kew. By Decimus Burton and Richard Turner, 1845–47. Exterior. Photo. J. R. Johnson.

XV 32   Palm Stove, Royal Botanic Gardens, Kew. By Decimus Burton and Richard Turner, 1845–47. Interior from *Illustrated London News*, 2 Sept. 1848.

XV 33   Palm Stove, Royal Botanic Gardens, Kew. By Decimus Burton and Richard Turner, 1845–47. Section and details from *Builder*, 15 Jan. 1848.

XV 34   Britannia Bridge, Menai Strait, Wales. By Robert Stephenson and Francis Thompson, 1845–50. From *Illustrated London News*, 23 Mar. 1850. (The Menai Bridge in the distance is by Thomas Telford, 1819–24).

XV 35   Britannia Bridge, Menai Strait, Wales. By Robert Stephenson and Francis Thompson, 1845–50. The Anglesey entrance, with lions by John Thomas, from Edwin Clark, *The Britannia and Conway Tubular Bridges*, 1850.

XV 36   Britannia Bridge, Menai Strait, Wales. By Robert Stephenson and Francis Thompson, 1845–50. Section of tube from Edwin Clark, *The Britannia and Conway Tubular Bridges*, 1850.

XV 37   Tubular Bridge, Conway, Wales. By Robert Stephenson and Francis Thompson, 1845–49. Floating the second tube into position to be hoisted, from Edwin Clark, *The Britannia and Conway Tubular Bridges*, 1850.

XV 38   Britannia Bridge, Menai Strait, Wales. By Robert Stephenson and Fran-

cis Thompson, 1845–50. Details of central pier from Edwin Clark, *The Britannia and Conway Tubular Bridges*, 1850.

XV 39   Chester and Holyhead Railway Station, Holywell, Wales. By Francis Thompson, 1847–48. From *Illustrated London News*, 19 Aug. 1848.

XV 40   Project for Light for All Nations on Goodwin Sands. By Bush, 1844–45. From *Illustrated London News*, 25 Jan. 1845.

XV 41   Prefabricated lighthouse for Bermuda. By Cottam and Hallen, 1843–44. (As first erected in Cornwall Rd., Southwark, London). From *Illustrated London News*, 20 Apr. 1844.

XV 42   General Station, Chester. By Robert Stephenson and Francis Thompson, 1844–48. Exterior from *Illustrated London News*, 19 Aug. 1848.

XV 43   General Station, Chester. By Robert Stephenson and Francis Thompson, 1844–48. Sheds from watercolor dated 1860 belonging to British Railways.

XV 44   Paragon Railway Station Hotel, Hull. By T. G. Andrews, 1847–48. Queen Victoria arriving. From *Illustrated London News*, 21 Oct. 1854.

XV 45   Central Station, Newcastle-on-Tyne. By John Dobson, 1846–50. Plan from *Civil Engineer and Architect's Journal*, 1848.

XV 46   Central Station, Newcastle-on-Tyne. By John Dobson, 1846–50. Sheds from drawing by Dobson in Charles Tomlinson, *The North-Eastern Railway*, Newcastle [1914].

XV 47   Eastern Counties Railway Station, London (Shoreditch II). By Sancton Wood, 1848–49. From *Illustrated London News*, 21 Dec. 1850.

XV 48   Sailors' Home, Canning Pl., Liverpool, 1846–49. Section, showing cast-iron galleries in court, from *Civil Engineer and Architect's Journal*, 17 May 1851.

XV 49   London and North-Western Railway Station, London (Euston II). By P. C. Hardwick, 1846–49. Great Hall from A. E. Richardson, *Monumental Classic Architecture* [1914].

XV 50   Sailors' Home, Canning Pl., Liverpool. By John Cunningham, 1846–49. Entrance gates. Photo. N.B.R.

XV 51   Prefabricated buildings awaiting shipment at Samuel Hemming's Clift-House Iron Building Works, near Bristol. From *Illustrated London News*, 18 Feb. 1854.

XV 52   Prefabricated iron and glazed terra cotta clock tower for Geelong, Australia. By James Edmeston, 1854. From *Illustrated London News*, 30 Dec. 1854.

XV 53   Prefabricated iron warehouse, with living rooms above, for export to San Francisco. By E. T. Bellhouse, 1850. From *Allgemeine Bauzeitung* (Vienna), 1850.

XV 54   Prefabricated iron ballroom, Balmoral Castle, near Ballater, Fifeshire. By E. T. Bellhouse, 1851. From *Illustrated London News*, 22 Nov. 1851.

XVI 1   "Official Design for the Edifice for the Great Exhibition of 1851." By

Building Committee of Royal Commission, 1850. From *Illustrated London News,* 22 June 1850.

XVI 2   First developed design for Crystal Palace I. By Sir Joseph Paxton, June 1850. As published in *Illustrated London News,* 6 July 1850.

XVI 3   Lily House, Chatsworth, Derbyshire. By Sir Joseph Paxton, 1849–50. Perspective and section from *Civil Engineer and Architect's Journal,* Aug., 1850.

XVI 4   Original sketch for Crystal Palace I. By Sir Joseph Paxton, middle of June 1850. From drawing at Royal Society of Arts.

XVI 5   Crystal Palace I, Hyde Park, London. By Sir Joseph Paxton, and Fox and Henderson, 1 Aug. 1850–1 May 1851. Trihedral view from lithograph by Ackerman and Co., 1851.

XVI 6   Crystal Palace, Hyde Park, London. By Sir Joseph Paxton, and Fox and Henderson, 1850–51. End view. Photo. Victoria and Albert Museum.

XVI 7   Crystal Palace, Hyde Park, London. By Sir Joseph Paxton, and Fox and Henderson, 1850–51. Standard bay elevation from Charles Downes, *The Building . . . for the Great Exhibition,* 1852.

XVI 8   Crystal Palace, Hyde Park, London. By Sir Joseph Paxton, and Fox and Henderson, 1850–51. Details of stanchions and girders from Charles Downes, *The Building . . . for the Great Exhibition,* 1852.

XVI 9   Crystal Palace, Hyde Park, London. By Sir Joseph Paxton, and Fox and Henderson, 1850–51. Looking across nave at gallery level. Photo. Victoria and Albert Museum.

XVI 10 Midland Station, Park End St., Oxford. By Fox and Henderson, 1851–52. Entrance porch and sheds. Photos. J. R. Johnson.

XVI 11 Sash-bar machine used at site during erection of Crystal Palace I, Hyde Park, London. From *Illustrated London News,* 23 Nov. 1850.

XVI 12 Early stage in construction of Crystal Palace I, Hyde Park, London. From *Illustrated London News,* 12 Oct. 1850.

XVI 13 Preparation of sub-assemblies at site for Crystal Palace I, Hyde Park, London. From *Illustrated London News,* 16 Nov. 1850.

XVI 14 Crystal Palace I in construction, Hyde Park, London. From *Illustrated London News,* 16 Nov. 1850.

XVI 15 Crystal Palace I, Hyde Park, London. By Sir Joseph Paxton, and Fox and Henderson, 1850–51. Transept with Sibthorp elm. Photo. Gernsheim Collection.

XVI 16 Crystal Palace I, Hyde Park, London. By Sir Joseph Paxton, and Fox and Henderson. Nave before installation of the exhibits. From *Builder,* 4 Jan. 1851.

XVI 17 Project for roofing court of Royal Exchange. By Sir Joseph Paxton, 1851. From *Civil Engineer and Architect's Journal,* 29 Mar. 1851.

XVI 18 Detailing by Owen Jones of staircase and gallery railings in Crystal Palace I. From Charles Downes, *The Building . . . for the Great Exhibition,* 1852.

XVI 19   Project for New York Crystal Palace. By Sir Joseph Paxton, 1852. From B. Silliman and C. R. Goodrich, *The World of Science, Art and Industry*, New York, 1854.

XVI 20   Project for reconstruction of Crystal Palace at Sydenham. By Sir Joseph Paxton, 1852. From drawing, signed by Paxton, in possession of Yale University.

XVI 21   Project for exercise-room, London Hospital for Diseases of the Chest, Victoria Park, London. By Sir Joseph Paxton, 1851. From *Illustrated London News*, 5 July 1851.

XVI 22   Crystal Palace, Merrion Sq. West, Dublin. By Sir John Benson, 1852–53. Exterior from *Illustrated London News*, 23 Oct. 1852.

XVI 23   Crystal Palace, Merrion Sq. West, Dublin. By Sir John Benson, 1852–53. Interior from *Illustrated London News*, 4 June 1853.

XVI 24   Crystal Palace II, Palace Parade, Sydenham. By Sir Joseph Paxton and Fox, Henderson and Co., 1852–54. Roof. Photo. Dell and Wainwright.

XVI 25   Project for extending Crystal Palace I. By Sir Joseph Paxton, 1852. From *Illustrated London News*, 1 May 1852.

XVI 26   Crystal Palace II, Palace Parade, Sydenham. By Sir Joseph Paxton, and Fox, Henderson and Co., 1852–54. Interior.

XVI 27   Lord Warden Railway Hotel, Dover. By Samuel Beazley, 1850–53. From *Illustrated London News*, 10 Sept. 1853.

XVI 28   Southerndown Hotel, near Bridgend, Glamorganshire. By J. P. Seddon, 1852–53. From *Builder*, 15 Jan. 1853.

XVI 29   Great Northern Railway Station, Euston Rd., London (King's Cross). By Lewis Cubitt, (1850) 1851–52. Plan from *Builder*, 2 Oct. 1852.

XVI 30   Great Northern Railway Station, Euston Rd., London (King's Cross). By Lewis Cubitt, (1850) 1851–52. Front of sheds on day of opening, 14 Oct. 1852, from drawing in possession of British Railways.

XVI 31   Great Northern Railway Station, Euston Rd., London (King's Cross). By Lewis Cubitt, (1850) 1851–52. Section of sheds from *Builder*, 2 Oct. 1852.

XVI 32   Great Northern Railway Station, Euston Rd., London (King's Cross). By Lewis Cubitt, (1850) 1851–52. Exterior. Photo. Thomas Spurge from British Railways.

XVI 33   Great Northern Railway Station, Euston Rd., London (King's Cross). By Lewis Cubitt, (1850) 1851–52. Laminated wooden arched trusses and cast-iron shoes. From *Builder*, 2 Oct. 1852.

XVI 34   Great Western Railway Station, Eastbourne Terrace, Paddington, London (Paddington II). By I. K. Brunel and M. D. Wyatt, 1852–54. One of "transepts" connecting the three sheds. Photo. J. R. Johnson.

XVI 35   Great Western Railway Station, Eastbourne Terrace, Paddington, London (Paddington II). By I. K. Brunel and M. D. Wyatt, 1852–54. Plan from British Railways.

XVI 36   Great Western Railway Station, Eastbourne Terrace, Paddington, Lon-

don (Paddington II). By I. K. Brunel and M. D. Wyatt, 1852–54. Sheds from *Illustrated London News,* 8 July 1854.

XVI 37 Great Western Railway Station, Eastbourne Terrace, Paddington, London (Paddington II). By I. K. Brunel and M. D. Wyatt, 1852–54. Interior wall of station block. Photo. R. H. de Burgh-Galwey.

XVI 38 "The Railway Station." By William P. Frith, 1861. From replica at Paddington Station.

XVI 39 Great Western Railway Station, Eastbourne Terrace, Paddington, London (Paddington II). By I. K. Brunel and M. D. Wyatt, 1852–54. Stationmaster's oriel. Photo. R. H. de Burgh-Galwey.

XVI 40 British Museum, Great Russell St., Bloomsbury, London. Reading Room by Sydney Smirke in construction, (1852) 1854–57. From *Illustrated London News,* 14 Apr. 1855.

XVI 41 Reading Room, British Museum, Great Russell St., Bloomsbury, London. By Sydney Smirke, (1852) 1854–57.

XVI 42 "The Aerial Ballet of the Brompton Boilermakers." (Museum of Science and Art, Brompton Park, London, by Young and Son, in construction, 1855–56.) Photo. Victoria and Albert Museum.

XVI 43 Museum of Science and Art, Brompton Park, London. By Young and Son, 1855–56. Sidewalls in construction. Photo. Victoria and Albert Museum.

XVI 44 Museum of Science and Art, Brompton Park, London. By Young and Son, 1855–56. Roof in construction. Photo. Victoria and Albert Museum.

XVI 45 Museum of Science and Art, Brompton Park, London. By Young and Son, 1855–56. Interior galleries before completion. Photo. Victoria and Albert Museum.

XVI 46 Museum of Science and Art, Brompton Park, London. By Young and Son, 1855–56. Interior at official opening from *Illustrated London News,* 12 Apr. 1856.

XVI 47 Museum of Science and Art, Brompton Park, London. By Young and Son, 1855–56. Entrance porch. Photo. Victoria and Albert Museum.

XVII 1 All Saints', Margaret St., Regent St., London. By William Butterfield, (1849) 1850–(1852)–1859. West front and tower. Photo. N.B.R.

XVII 2 All Saints', Margaret St., Regent St., London. By William Butterfield, (1849) 1850–(1852)–1859. First published view of exterior from *Builder,* 22 Jan. 1853.

XVII 3 All Saints', Margaret St., Regent St., London. By William Butterfield, (1849) 1850–(1852)–1859. South buttress with "Annunciation" relief. Photo. N.B.R.

XVII 4 All Saints', Margaret St., Regent St., London. By William Butterfield, (1849) 1850–(1852)–1859. Juxtaposition of south porch, tower shaft and choir school. Photo. N.B.R.

XVII 5   All Saints', Margaret St., Regent St., London. By William Butterfield, (1849) 1850-(1852)-1859. Interior from *Builder*, 4 June 1859.

XVII 6   All Saints', Margaret St., Regent St., London. By William Butterfield, (1849) 1850-(1852)-1859. Nave arcade and chancel arch. Photo. N.B.R.

XVII 7   All Saints', Margaret St., Regent St., London. By William Butterfield, (1849) 1850-(1852)-1859. South aisle. Photo. N.B.R.

XVII 8   All Saints', Margaret St., Regent St., London. By William Butterfield, (1849) 1850-(1852)-1859. Plan from *Builder*, 22 Jan. 1853.

XVII 9   All Saints', Margaret St., Regent St., London. By William Butterfield, (1849) 1850-(1852)-1859. Interior looking east. Photo. N.B.R.

XVII 10   Choir school and clergy house of All Saints', Margaret St., Regent St., London. By William Butterfield, (1849) 1850-(1852)-1859. Photo. N.B.R.

XVII 11   All Saints', Margaret St., Regent St., London. By William Butterfield, (1849) 1850-(1852)-1859. North wall of chancel. Photo. N.B.R.

XVII 12   St. Thomas's, Melbourne St., Leeds. By William Butterfield, 1850-52. Photo. Courtesy of John Summerson.

XVII 13   Original project for St. Matthias's, Stoke Newington, London. By William Butterfield, 1850. From *Ecclesiologist*, Vol. 11.

XVII 14   St. Matthias's, Howard Rd., Stoke Newington, London. By William Butterfield, (1850) 1851-53. East end after blitz. Photo. Dell and Wainwright.

XVII 15   St. Matthias's, Howard Rd., Stoke Newington, London. By William Butterfield, (1850) 1851-53. West front after blitz. Photo. Dell and Wainwright.

I THE STUDY OF VICTORIAN ARCHITECTURE

I 1 *Westminster New Palace, London. By Sir Charles Barry, A. N. W. Pugin, and E. M. Barry. Original design 1835–36; executed 1840–c.1865.*

I 2 *Athenaeum, Mosley St., Manchester. By Sir Charles Barry, 1837–39.*

I 3 *Barry's original design for Athenaeum, 1836.*

I 4   St. Mary's, Southwark,
London. By Benjamin Ferrey,
1840–41.

I 5   St. Agatha's, Llanymynech,
Shropshire. By R. K. Penson,
1842–44.

I 6   Design for "Swiss Chalet."
By P. F. Robinson, 1827.

I 7   Highclere Castle, Hampshire.
By Sir Charles Barry, (1837) 1842–c.1855.

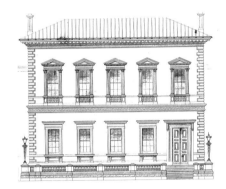

I 8   Travellers' Club House, Pall Mall, London.
By Sir Charles Barry, (1829) 1830–32.

I 9   Harlaxton Hall, Lincolnshire.
By Anthony Salvin, 1834–c.1855.
(Photo Country Life.)

II THE 1830'S

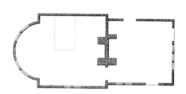

II 1   "Pleasure Cottage." By James Malton, 1798. Exterior and plan.

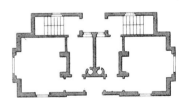

II 2   "Rustic Double Cottage." By Sir John Soane, 1798. Exterior and plan.

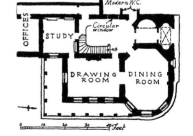

II 3   Cronkhill, near Shrewsbury. By John Nash, c.1802. Exterior and plan.

II 4 *"Four Cottages." By Joseph Gandy, 1805.*

II 5 *"Italian Villa." By Robert Lugar, 1805.*

II 6 *"Double Cottage." By Robert Lugar, 1805. Elevation and plan.*

II 7 Gwrych Castle,
near Abergele,
Denbighshire, Wales.
By C. A. Busby and (?)
Lloyd Bamford Hesketh,
c.1814.

II 8 Italian Villa.
By J. B. Papworth, 1818.

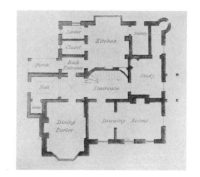

II 9 *"Vicarage House." By J. B. Papworth, 1818.*
Elevation and plan.

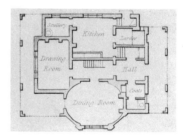

II 10 *"Cottage Ornée." By J. B. Papworth,*
1818. Perspective and plan.

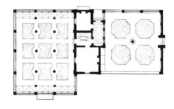

II 11 *Lodge, Villa Borghese, Rome.*
From Charles Parker's Villa rustica, *1832.*
Perspective and plan.

II 12   "Gothic Villa." By E. B. Lamb, 1833.

II 13   "Gothic Villa." By E. B. Lamb, 1836.

II 14   "Italian Villa." By E. B. Lamb, 1836.

II 15   "Villa in the Cottage Style."
By Francis Goodwin, c.1834.

II 16   "Country Public House."
By E. B. Lamb, 1833.

II 17   Royal Institution (now City Art Gallery), Manchester. By Sir Charles Barry, (1824) 1827–35.

II 18   St. Peter's Parish Church, Brighton.
By Sir Charles Barry, (1823) 1824–28.

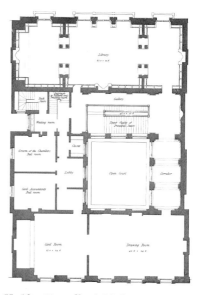

II 19   Travellers' Club House, London.
By Sir Charles Barry, (1829) 1830–32.
Garden front and plan.

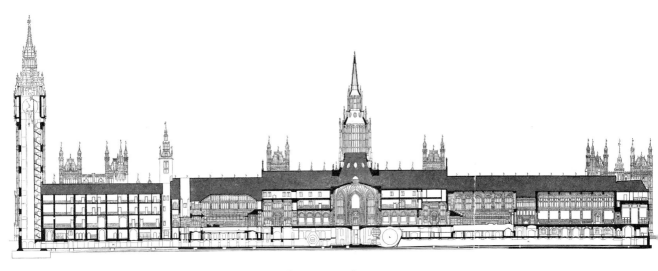

*II 20 Westminster New Palace, London. By Sir Charles Barry and
A. N. W. Pugin, (1835–36) 1840–c.1865. Longitudinal section.*

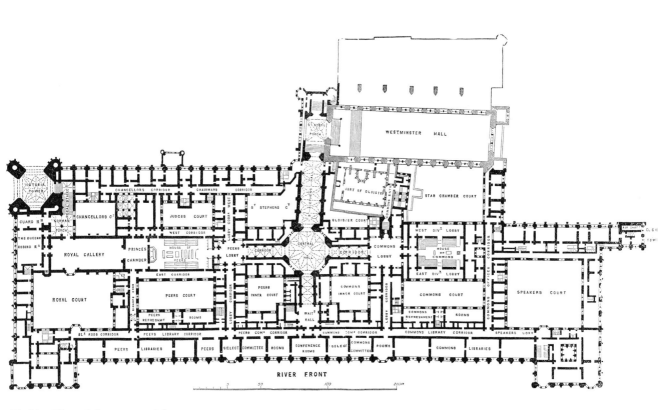

II 21 Plan of the principal floor.

II 22   Original design, south elevation.

II 23   Original design, north elevation.

II 24 *Original design for Westminster New Palace, London.*
By Sir Charles Barry and A. N. W. Pugin, c.1836. West elevation.

II 25 *Perspective of river front as projected, 1836.*

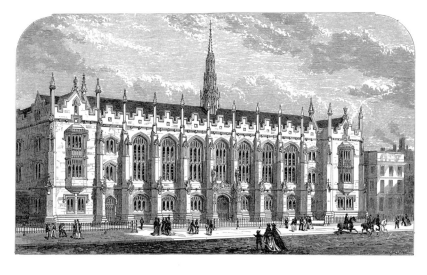

II 26 *King Edward's*
Free Grammar School,
New St., Birmingham.
By Sir Charles Barry,
(1833) 1834–37.

III PUGIN AS A CHURCH ARCHITECT

III 1   Our Lady, Lisson Grove, London.
By J. J. Scoles, 1833–34.

III 2   "Contrasted Public Inns," from
A. N. W. Pugin's Contrasts, 1836.

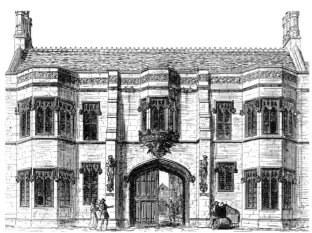

III 3   Norman church.
By G. E. Hamilton, 1836.

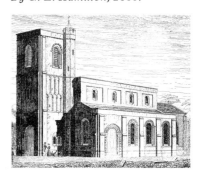

III 4   St. Augustine's,
Tunbridge Wells.
By Joseph Ireland, 1837–38.

III 5   St. Clement's, Oxford.
Architect and date unknown.

III 6   St. Marie's, Bridgegate, Derby.
By A. N. W. Pugin, 1838–39. West front.

III 7   Interior (painted decoration renewed 1930).

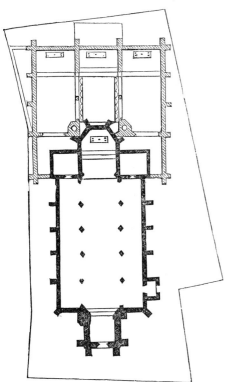

III 8   Plan, with indication
of projected eastward extension.

III 9   Nave arcade and clerestorey.

III 10 *The churches of A. N. W. Pugin,*
from his Apology for the Revival, *1843.*

1. *St. George's, Southwark, London*
2. *St. Peter's, Woolwich*
3. *St. Marie's, Stockton-on-Tees*
4. *St. Giles's, Cheadle*
5. *St. Marie's, Newcastle-on-Tyne*
6. *North Gate, St. Marie's, Oscott*
7. *St. Austin's, Kenilworth*
8. *Jesus Chapel, Pomfret*
9. *Cathedral, Killarney*
10. *St. Chad's, Birmingham*
11. *St. Oswald's,*
    Old Swan, Liverpool
12. *Holy Cross, Kirkham*
13. *St. Barnabas's, Nottingham*
14. *St. Michael Archangel's,*
    Gorey, Ireland
15. *St. Marie's, Derby*
16. *St. Alban's, Macclesfield*
17. *St. Marie's, Brewood*
18. *St. Winifride's, Shepshead*
19. *St. Andrew's, Cambridge*
20. *St. Bernard's Abbey, Coalville*
21. *St. Marie's, Keighley*
22. *St. Marie's, Warwick Bridge*
23. *St. Wilfrid's,*
    Hulme, Manchester
24. *St. Marie's, Southport*
25. *St. John's Hospital, Alton*

III 11 St. George's, Lambeth Rd., Southwark, London.
By A. N. W. Pugin, 1840–48. Interior after blitz.

III 12 Project for St. George's,
Southwark, 1838.

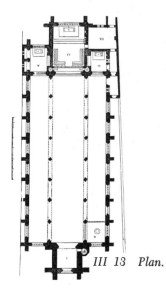

III 13 Plan.

III 14 Project for St. George's, Southwark. Interior.

III 15   Bishop Ryder's Church,
Gem St., Birmingham. By Rickman and
Hussey, 1837–38.

III 16   St. Chad's, Bath St.,
Birmingham. By A. N. W. Pugin, 1839–41.
Exterior (with modern northwest chapel).

III 17   St. Chad's, Birmingham. Interior.

III 18   St. Chad's, Birmingham. West front.

III 19   St. Wilfrid's, Hulme, Manchester. By A. N. W. Pugin, 1839–42. Perspective and plan.

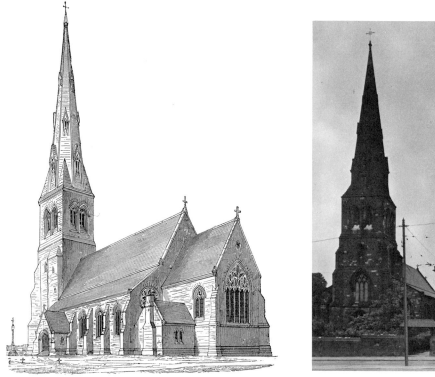

III 20   St. Oswald's, Old Swan, Liverpool. By A. N. W. Pugin, 1840–42.
Perspective from southeast and west front with school.

III 21 "*Contrasted Residences of the Poor,*" *from A. N. W. Pugin's* Contrasts, *2d ed. 1841.*

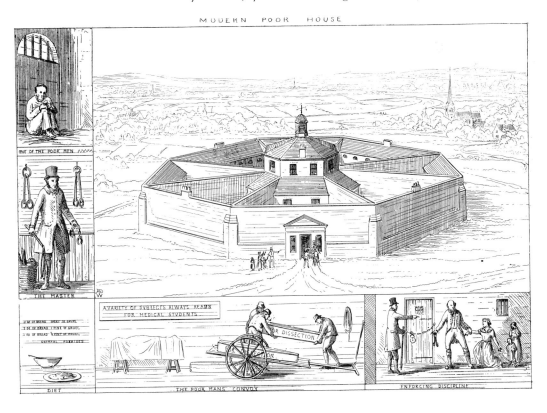

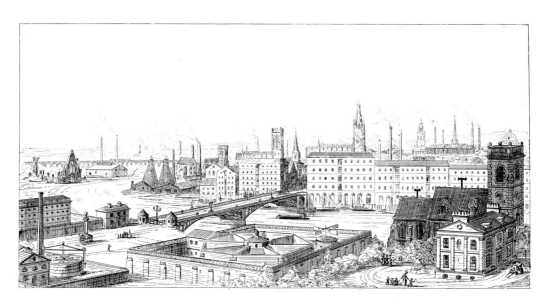

III 22 *"Contrasted English Towns, 1840 and 1440," from A. N. W. Pugin's* Contrasts, *2d ed. 1841*.

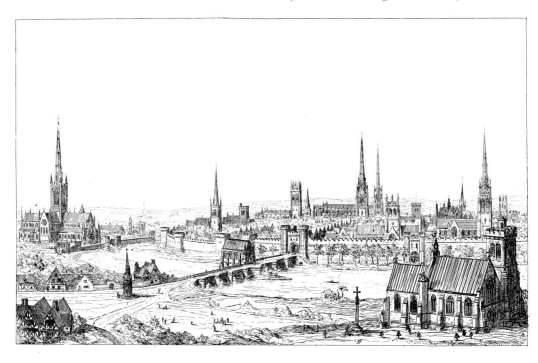

III 23 *St. Mary's, Stockton-on-Tees, Co. Durham. By A. N. W. Pugin, 1840–42.*

III 24 *An ideal medieval parish church, from A. N. W. Pugin's* True Principles, *1841.*

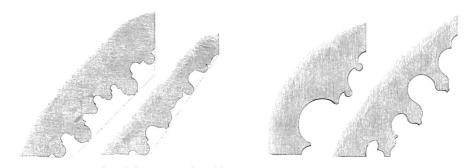

III 25 *Approved and disapproved moldings, from A. N. W. Pugin's* True Principles, *1841.*

III 27   Interior.

III 26   St. Giles's, Cheadle, Staffordshire.
By A. N. W. Pugin, 1841–46.
Above, exterior from northeast; below, plan.

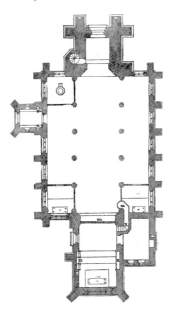

III 28   Interior, showing chancel screen.

III 29 St. Barnabas's, Derby Rd., Nottingham.
By A. N. W. Pugin, 1842–44.
Projected chancel decorations.

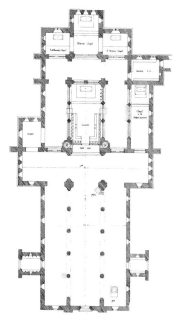

III 30 Plan.

III 31 Nave looking east.

III 32 Exterior from northeast.

III 33 Exterior from south.

III 34   St. Augustine's, West Cliff, Ramsgate, Kent.
By A. N. W. Pugin, 1846–51. Interior, looking east from south transept.

III 35   St. Augustine's. Exterior from southeast.

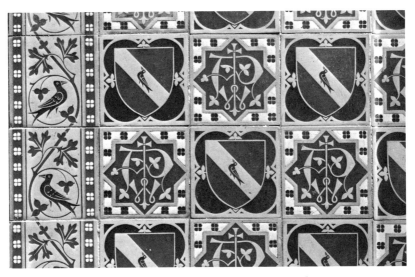

III 36   St. Augustine's. Floor tiles with Pugin's arms and monogram.

III 37   Our Lady of Victories, Clapham Park Rd.,
London. By W. W. Wardell, 1849–52.

III 40   Church of the Holy Apostles, Clifton Rd.,
Bristol. Interior, 1847–49. Architect unknown.

III 38   St. John's, White Cross
Bank, Salford. By Hadfield and
Weightman, 1844–48.

III 39   Immaculate Conception,
Farm St., Grosvenor Square,
London. By J. J. Scoles, 1844–49.

III 41   St. Raphael's, Kingston-
on-Thames, Surrey. By Charles
Parker, 1846–47.

IV ANGLICAN AND

NON-CONFORMIST CHURCHES

OF THE LATE 30'S AND

EARLY 40'S

IV 1   Holy Trinity,
Blackheath Hill, London.
By J. W. Wild, 1838–39.

IV 2   St. Paul's, Valetta,
Malta. Begun 1839.

IV 3   St. Laurence's, Southampton. By J. W. Wild, 1839.

IV 4   St. Peter's Parish Church, Kirkgate, Leeds.
By R. D. Chantrell, 1839–41. Exterior from northeast.

IV 5   Interior.

IV 6   Ss. Mary and Nicholas's, Wilton, Wiltshire.
By Wyatt and Brandon, 1840–46. West front.

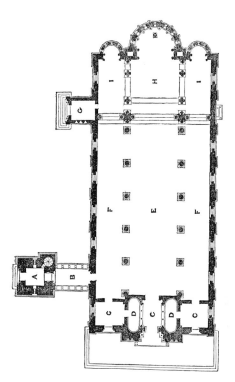

IV 7   Ss. Mary and Nicholas's. Plan.

IV 8   Ss. Mary and Nicholas's. Interior.

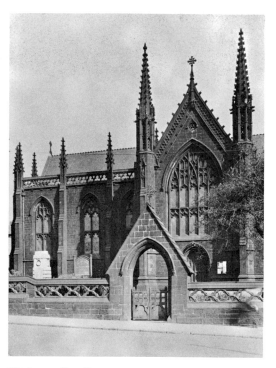

IV 9   Mill Hill Unitarian Chapel, Park Row,
Leeds. By Bowman and Crowther, 1847–48.

IV 10   Christ Church, Streatham, London. By J. W. Wild, 1840–42.

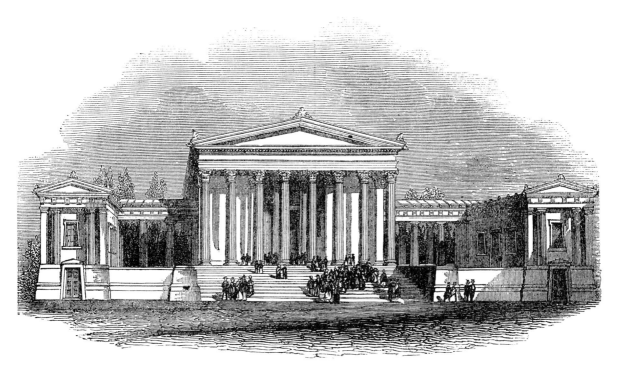

IV 11 *Great Thornton Street Chapel, Hull. By Lockwood and Allom, 1843.*

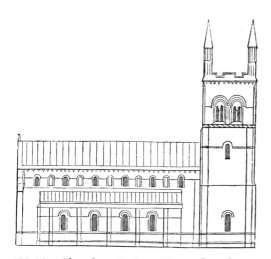

IV 12 *Church at Scofton, Nottinghamshire. By Ambrose Poynter, c.1840. From Charles Anderson's* Ancient Models, *new ed. 1841.*

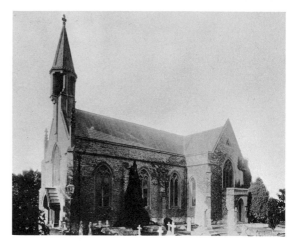

IV 13 *St. Matthew's, Otterbourne, Hampshire. By W. C. Yonge, c.1840.*

IV 14 St. Jude's, Manningham, Bradford. By Walker Rawstone, 1841–43.

IV 15 St. Jude's, Old Bethnal Green Rd., London. By Henry Clutton, 1844–46. Interior after blitz.

IV 16 All Saints' Parish Church, Leamington, Warwickshire. By the Reverend John Craig, 1843–49.

IV 17 St. Saviour's, Cavalier Hill, Leeds.
By J. M. Derick, 1842–45.

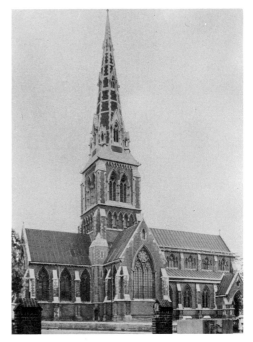

IV 19 St. Giles's, Camberwell Church St.,
London. By Scott and
Moffatt, 1842–44. Exterior from north.

IV 18 Christ Church, Endell St., London.
By Benjamin Ferrey, 1842–44.

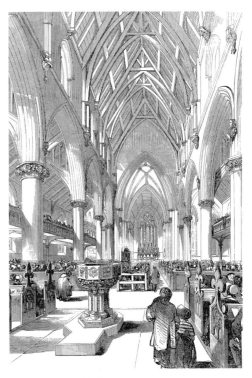

IV 20 St. Giles's. Interior.

IV 21 Memorial Church, Colabah,
India. By J. M. Derick, c.1844.

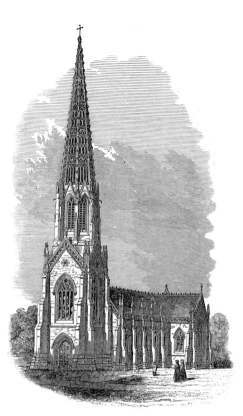

IV 22 St. Stephen's, Lever Bridge, Bolton-
le-Moors. By Edmund Sharpe, 1842–45.

IV 23 Holy Trinity, Gloucester Terrace,
Paddington, London.
By Thomas Cundy II, 1844–46.

IV 24 Martyrs' Memorial,
St. Giles St., Oxford.
By Sir G. G. Scott, 1841.

IV 25   Holy Trinity, Rusholme, Manchester.
By Edmund Sharpe, 1844–46.

IV 26   St. Alkmund's, Bridgegate, Derby.
By I. H. Stevens, 1844–46.

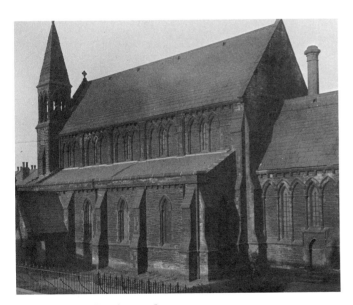

IV 27   St. Andrew's, Leeds.
By Scott and Moffatt, 1844–45.

IV 28   St. Mark's, Swindon, Berkshire.
By Scott and Moffatt, 1843–45.

IV 29 Walter Scott Monument, East Prince's St. Gardens, Edinburgh. By E. Meikle Kemp, (1836) 1840–46.

V ANGLICAN AND NON-CONFORMIST

CHURCHES OF THE LATE 40'S

V 1 *Clapham Congregational Church, Grafton Sq.,*
London. By John Tarring, 1850–52.

V 2 *Cavendish Street Independent Chapel,*
Manchester. By Edward Walters, 1847–48.

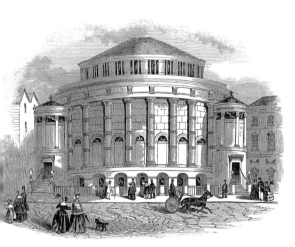

V 3 *Particular Baptist Chapel, Belvoir St.,*
Leicester. By J. A. Hansom, 1844–45.

V 4 *Central Baptist Chapel, Bloomsbury St.,*
London. By John Gibson, 1845–48.

V 5 *Accepted design for Nikolaikirche,*
Hamburg. By Sir G. G. Scott, (1844) 1845–63.

V 6 *St. Andrew's, Wells St.,*
London. By Dawkes and Hamilton, 1845–47.

V 7 *St. Matthew's, City Road, London. By*
Sir G. G. Scott and (?) G. E. Street, 1847–48.

V 8 *Independent Church, Glasgow.*
By J. T. Emmett, 1852.

V 9 St. Peter's, Tewksbury Rd., Cheltenham.
By S. W. Dawkes, 1847–49. Exterior, from southeast.

V 10   St. Peter's. Interior.

V 11   St. Ann's, New St., Alderney.
By Sir G. G. Scott, 1847–50.

V 12   St. Matthias's, Chilton St., London.
By Wyatt and Brandon, 1847–48

V 13   St. Saviour's Vicarage, Coalpitheath,
Gloucestershire. By William Butterfield, 1844–45.

V 14   Lychgate, St. Saviour's Churchyard,
Coalpitheath, Gloucestershire.
By William Butterfield, 1844–45.

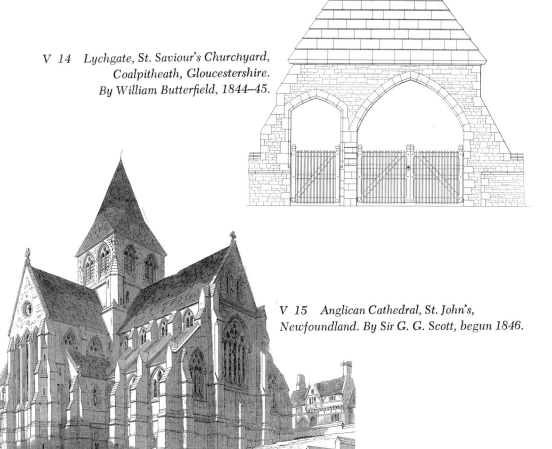

V 15   Anglican Cathedral, St. John's,
Newfoundland. By Sir G. G. Scott, begun 1846.

V 16   *Original design for St. Mary Magdalene's, Munster Sq., London. By R. C. Carpenter, 1849.*

V 17   *Interior.*

V 18   *St. Paul's, Manningham, Bradford. By Mallinson and Healey, 1847–48.*

V 19   *St. Thomas's, Winchester. By E. W. Elmslie, (1844) 1845–46 (tower completed 1856–57).*

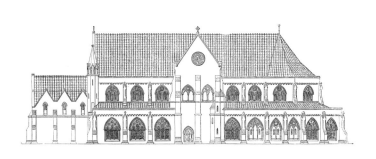

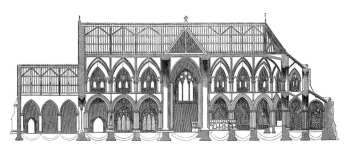

V 20   Design for Anglican Cathedral, Colombo, Ceylon.
By R. C. Carpenter, 1847. Side elevation and section.

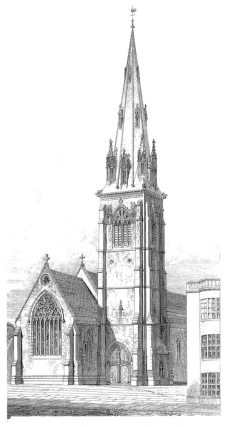

V 21   Original design for St. Paul's, West St.,
Brighton. By R. C. Carpenter, 1846–48.

V 22   St. Paul's. Interior.

V 23   St. Paul's. East portal.

V 24 *St. John's College, Hurstpierpoint, Sussex. By R. C. Carpenter, 1851–53.*

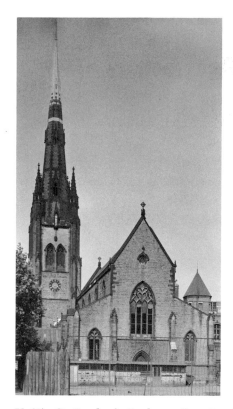

V 25 *St. Stephen's, Rochester Row, London. By Benjamin Ferrey, 1847–50.* V 26 *Interior.*

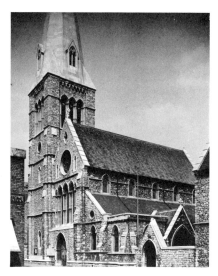

V 27 St. Barnabas's, Pimlico,
London. By Thomas Cundy II and (?)
William Butterfield, 1846–50.

V 28 St. Barnabas's. Clergy House.

V 29 St. Barnabas's. Interior.

V 30 Holy Trinity, Bessborough
Gardens, London.
By J. L. Pearson, 1849–52.

V 31 *Independent Chapel, Boston.
By Stephen Lewin, 1849–50.*

V 33 *St. Thomas's, Coventry. By Sharpe and Paley,
1848–49. Exterior, from northwest.*

V 32 *All Saints', Thirkleby,
Yorkshire. By E. B. Lamb, 1848–50.*

V 34 *Interior.*

V 35 *Catholic Apostolic Church, Gordon Sq., London.*
By Brandon and Ritchie, 1850–54. Exterior from north.

V 36 *Interior.*

V 37   *Caledonia Rd. Free Church, Glasgow. By Alexander Thomson, 1856–57.*

VI   BARRY AS AN ARCHITECT OF ''PALACES''

VI 1   *Italian Gardens, Trentham Park, near Stoke-on-Trent. By Sir Charles Barry and W. A. Nesfield, c.1835–40.*

VI 2   *Trentham Park as altered by Sir Charles Barry, c.1835–c.1850. (Photo Country Life.)*

VI 3 *Town Hall, Crossley St., Halifax. By Sir Charles Barry and E. M. Barry, (1859) 1860–62.*

VI 4 *Reform Club House, Pall Mall, London. By Sir Charles Barry, (1837) 1838–40. Elevation.* VI 5 *Plan.*

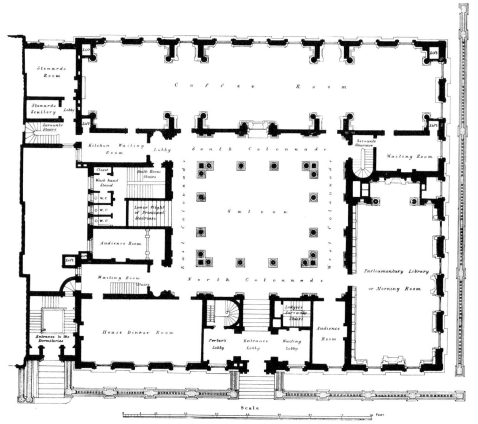

VI 6 *Reform Club House. North front, with Travellers' Club House beyond.*

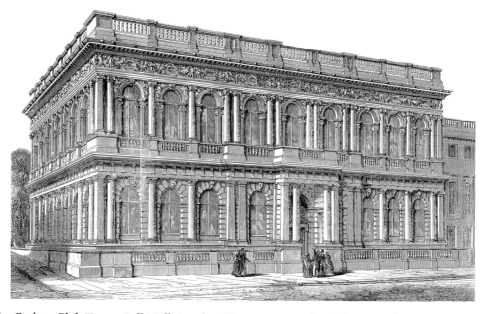

VI 7 *Carlton Club House, Pall Mall, London. Winning project by Sydney Smirke for new front, 1847.*

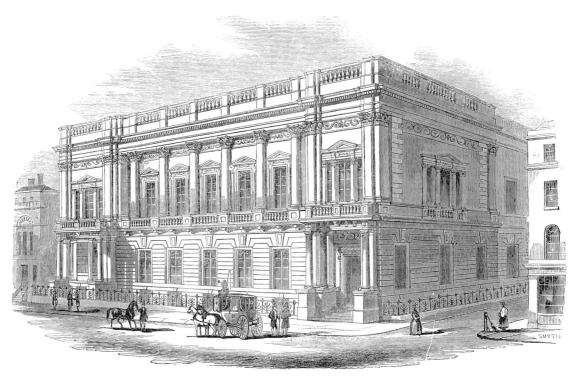

VI 8 *Conservative Club House, St. James's St., London. By George Basevi and Sydney Smirke, 1843–44.*

VI 9 *Army and Navy Club House, Pall Mall, London. By Parnell and Smith, 1848–51.*

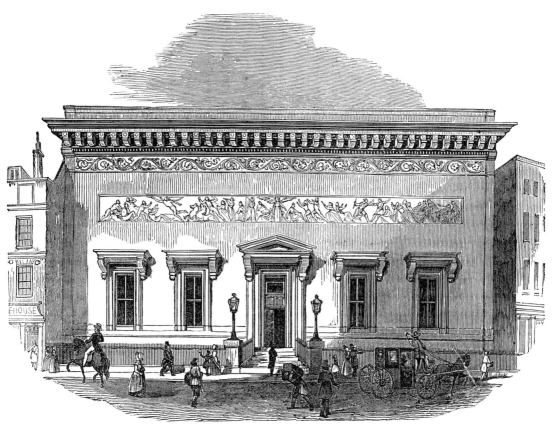

VI 10 *Moxhay's Hall of Commerce, Threadneedle St., London, 1842–43.*

VI 11 *Hall of Physicians, Queen St.,*
Edinburgh. By Thomas Hamilton, 1844–45.

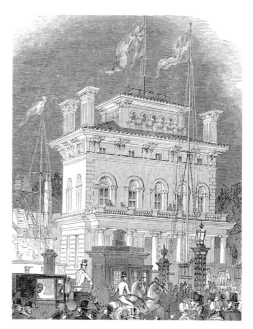

VI 12 *Southampton Yacht Club,*
Southampton. By T. S. Hack, 1845.

VI 13 *Mansion, Kensington Palace Gardens, London. By J. T. Knowles, 1847.*

VI 16 *Plymouth and Cottonian Libraries, Plymouth. By George Wightwick, 1851–52. Front elevation.*

VI 17 *British Embassy, Constantinople. By Sir Charles Barry and W. J. Smith, (1842) 1845–47.*

VI 14 *Hudson Mansion, Albert Gate, London. By Thomas Cubitt, 1843–45. (Conservatory not original.)*

VI 15 *Athenaeum, Sheffield. By George Alexander, 1847–48.*

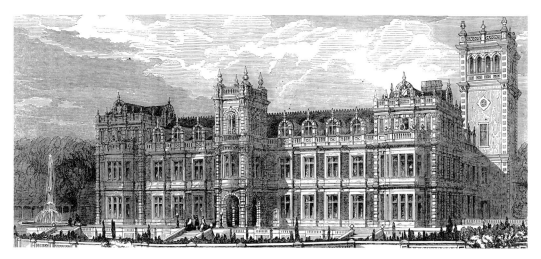

VI 18   *Somerleyton Hall, near Lowestoft. As refaced by John Thomas, 1844–51.*

VI 19   *Highclere Castle, near Burghclere, Hampshire. As refaced by Sir Charles Barry, (1837) 1842–44.*

VI 20   *Athenaeum, Bury, Lancashire. By Sydney Smirke, 1850–51.*

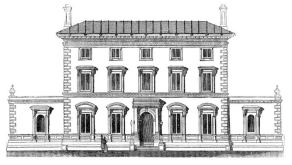

VI 21   *Mansion, Kensington Palace Gardens, London. By R. R. Banks, 1845.*

VI 22 *Osborne House, near East Cowes, Isle of Wight. By Prince Albert and Thomas Cubitt. Private pavilion, 1845–46.* VI 23 *Garden front, 1847–49.*

VI 24 *Harlaxton Hall. By Anthony Salvin, 1834–c.1855. (Photo Country Life.)*

VII THE BARRY STORY CONTINUED

VII 1   *City of London Prison, Camden Rd., London. By J. B. Bunning, 1851–52.*

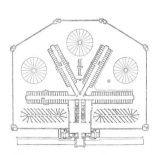   

VII 2   *Pentonville Prison, London. By Sir Charles Barry, 1841–43. Plan.*   VII 3   *Entrance block.*

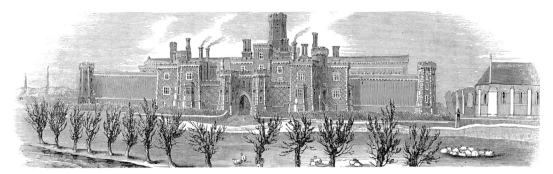

VII 4   *Berkshire County Gaol, Reading. By Scott and Moffatt, 1842–44.*

VII 5   *Dunrobin Castle, Sutherlandshire. By Sir Charles Barry and Leslie of Aberdeen, (1844) 1845–48.*

VII 6   *Board of Trade, Whitehall, London. By Sir Charles Barry, 1845–47.*

VII 7   *Bridgewater House, Cleveland Sq., London. By Sir Charles Barry, 1847–57. Entrance front.*

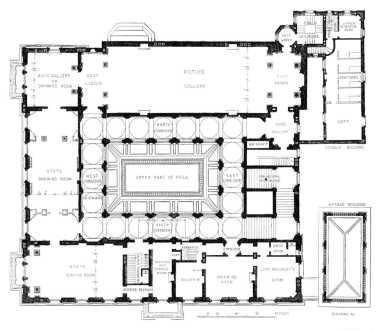

VII 8   *Bridgewater House. Plan.*

VII 9   *Ceiling in large drawing room.*

VII 10   *Bridgewater House. Green Park front.*

VII 11   *Bridgewater House. Doorcase in large drawing room.*

VII 12   *Picture Gallery after blitz.*

VII 13   *Dorchester House, Park Lane, London. By Lewis Vulliamy, 1848–63. Park front.*

VII 14   *Dorchester House. Plan.*

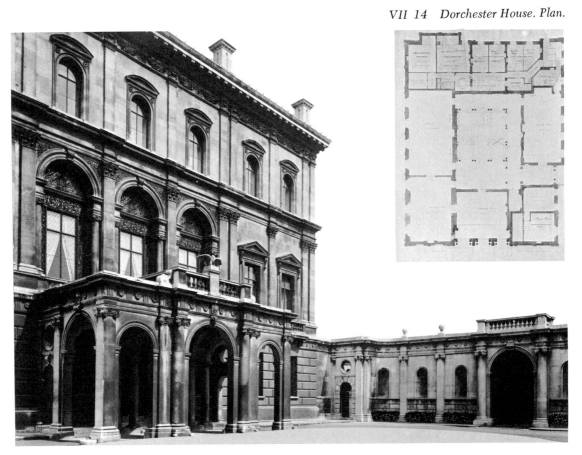

VII 15   *Dorchester House. Entrance court.*

VII 16   *Great Western Hotel, Paddington, London. By P. C. Hardwick, 1851–53.*

VII 17   *Henry Thomas Hope House, Piccadilly at Down St., London. By P. C. Dusillon and T. L. Donaldson, 1848–51.*

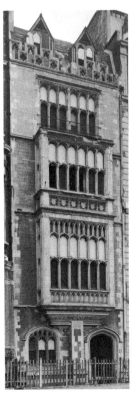

VII 18   *Charles Russell House, 23 Park Lane, London. By W. B. Moffatt, 1846–48.*

VII 19 General Hospital,
Bristol. By W. B. Gingell,
(1852) 1853–57.

VII 20 Shrubland Park,
near Ipswich. As remodeled by
Sir Charles Barry, 1848–50.

VII 21 Cliveden, near
Maidenhead. By Sir
Charles Barry, 1849–51.
(Photo Country Life.)

VIII MANORIAL AND

CASTELLATED COUNTRY HOUSES

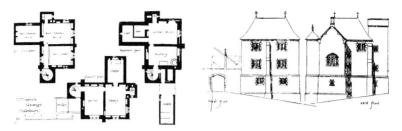

VIII 1   St. Marie's Grange, near Salisbury. By A. N. W. Pugin,
1835–36. Plans and elevations.

VIII 2   Project for additions to Scarisbrick Hall, Lancashire.
By A. N. W. Pugin, 1837.

VIII 3   Scarisbrick Hall, near Ormskirk, Lancashire.
As remodeled by A. N. W. Pugin, 1837–52, and E. W. Pugin, 1860–68.

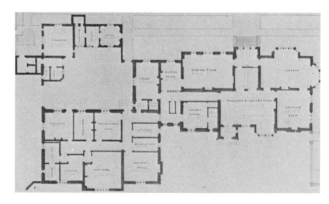

VIII 4 *Scotney Castle,*
Lamberthurst, Kent.
By Anthony Salvin, 1837–40.
Entrance front (above)
and plan (right).
(Photo Country Life.)

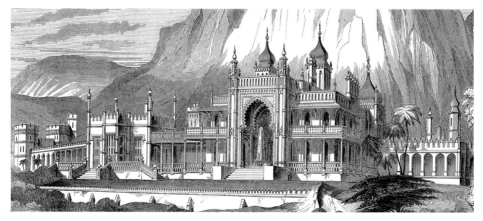

VIII 5   *Alupka, near Yalta, Crimea. By Edward Blore, 1837–40.*

VIII 6   *Ramsey Abbey, Huntingdonshire. By Edward Blore, 1838–39.*

VIII 7   *Worsley Hall, Eccles, near Manchester.*
By Edward Blore, (1839) 1840–45.
Perspective and plan.

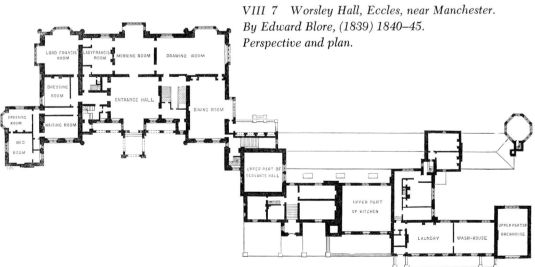

VIII 8 *Wray Castle, Lake Windermere.*
By Horner of Liverpool, 1840–47.

VIII 9 *Alton Castle, Staffordshire.*
Rebuilt by A. N. W. Pugin, c.1840.

VIII 10 *St. Marie's Presbytery, Bridgegate,*
Derby. By A. N. W. Pugin, c.1840.

VIII 11 *Convent of Sisters of Mercy, Hunter Rd.,*
Birmingham. By A. N. W. Pugin, 1840–41.

VIII 12   Alton Towers, Staffordshire. Exterior of hall by A. N. W. Pugin, 1849.

VIII 13   Bilton Grange, near Rugby. By A. N. W. Pugin, 1841–46.

VIII 14   The Grange, West Cliff, Ramsgate. By A. N. W. Pugin, 1841–43.

VIII 15   *Tortworth Court, Cromhall, Gloucestershire. By S. S. Teulon, 1849–53. Perspective and plan.*

VIII 16   *Enbrook, near Folkestone. By S. S. Teulon, 1853–55.*   VIII 17   *Plan.*

VIII 18   *Aldermaston Court, near Newbury. By P. C. Hardwick, 1848–51. (Photo Country Life.)*

VIII 19   Peckforton Castle, Cheshire. By Anthony Salvin, 1846–50. Corps de logis.

VIII 20   Peckforton Castle.

VIII 21   Peckforton Castle. Inside the court.

VIII 22 *Lismore Castle, near Waterford, Ireland. By Sir Joseph Paxton and G. H. Stokes, 1850–57.*

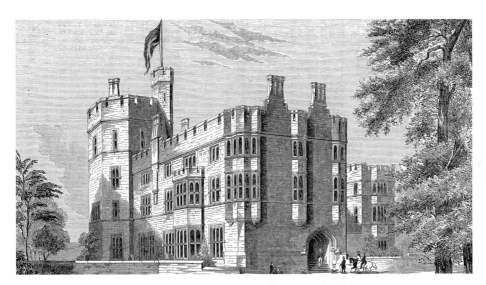

VIII 23 *Ruthin Castle, Denbighshire. By Henry Clutton, 1851–53.*

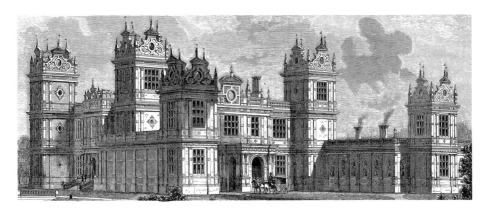

VIII 24 *Mentmore, near Cheddington, Buckinghamshire. By Sir Joseph Paxton and G. H. Stokes, 1852–54.*

VIII 26   Balmoral Castle I.
By William Smith, c.1845.

VIII 27   Balmoral Castle III. Garden front.

VIII 25 *Balmoral Castle III,*
near Ballater, Fifeshire.
By William Smith of Aberdeen
and Prince Albert, 1853–55.
The front entrance.

VIII 28 *Balmoral Castle III.*
Distant view.

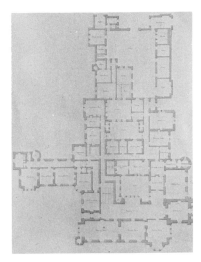

VIII 29   *Buchanan House, near Glasgow. By William Burn, 1851–54. Perspective and plan.*

VIII 30   *Project for Fonthill House, near Hinton, Wiltshire. By William Burn, c.1847–52.*

VIII 31   *Fonthill House, c.1847–52. (Photo Country Life.)*

VIII 32 *Clonghanadfoy Castle, near Limerick, Ireland. By G. F. Jones of York, c.1848–50.*

VIII 33 *Balentore, Scotland. By William Burn, c.1850.*

VIII 34 *Bylaugh Hall,*
near East Dereham, Norfolk.
By Banks and Barry, 1849–52.

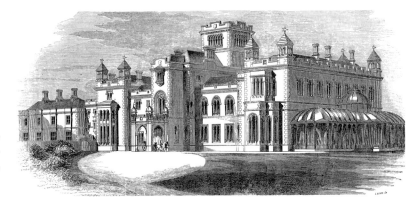

VIII 35 *Grittleton House,*
near Chippenham, Wiltshire.
By James Thomson, c.1845–60.

VIII 36 *Vinters, near*
Maidstone. As remodeled by
C. J. Richardson, 1850.

IX ROYAL AND STATE PATRONAGE

IX 1   *Buckingham Palace, London. East front by Edward Blore, 1846–48.*

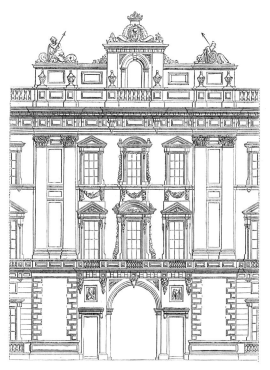

IX 2   *Central Pavilion.*

IX 3   *Chapel. By Edward Blore, 1842–43.*

IX 4   Ballroom. By Sir James Pennethorne, 1852–55.

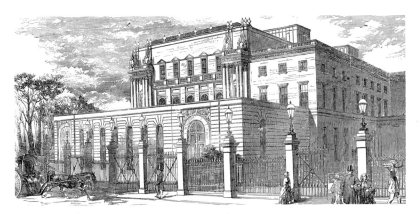

IX 5   South wing. By Sir James Pennethorne, 1852–55.

IX 6   Supper Room. By Sir James Pennethorne, 1852–55.

IX 7 St. Stephen's Cloisters,
Westminster New Palace, London.
Built c.1526–29 but restored by
Sir Charles Barry and A. N. W. Pugin.

IX 8 Westminster New Palace, London. By Sir Charles Barry and A. N. W. Pugin.
The House of Lords, 1840–46.

IX 9 Peers' Lobby, 1840–46.

IX 10   *Queen Victoria on throne in House of Lords receiving Speech from*
Lord Chancellor at Opening of Parliament.

IX 11 *Exterior of House of Lords, 1840–46.*

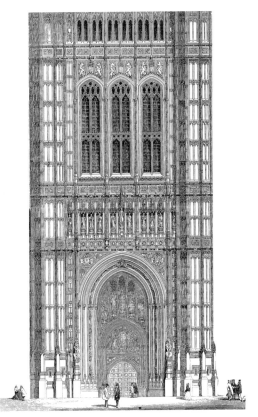

IX 12 *Westminster New Palace, London.*
Lower stages of Victoria Tower, 1840–52.

IX 13 *House of Commons. As first completed, 1840–49.*

IX 14   House of Commons.
As remodeled, 1850–51.

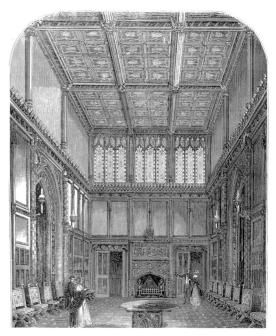

IX 15   Victoria Lobby. 1840–46.

IX 16   Queen Victoria entering
Royal Staircase.

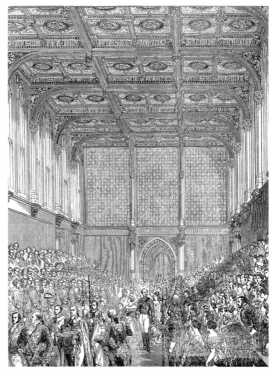

IX 17   Victoria Gallery, with Queen
Victoria approaching House of Lords.

IX 18 Westminster New Palace.
Central Octagon.
(Before installation of mosaics.)

IX 19 St. Stephen's Hall.

IX 20 St. Stephen's Porch and portion of west front.
(Porch completed after Pugin's death in 1852 but before 1856.)

IX 21   Westminster Hall, London.
11th–14th centuries. St.
Stephen's Porch at the end by Sir
Charles Barry and A. N. W. Pugin.

IX 22   Westminster New Palace.
Library of House of
Lords. As completed, c.1852.

IX 23   Westminster New Palace. Roofs seen from Victoria Tower,
with lantern over Central Octagon in foreground and Clock Tower to rear.

IX 24 *Westminster New Palace.*
Top of Victoria Tower as projected
by Barry before his death in 1860.

IX 25 *Westminster New Palace.*
By Sir Charles Barry and A. N. W. Pugin.
Belfry of Clock Tower in construction, 1857.

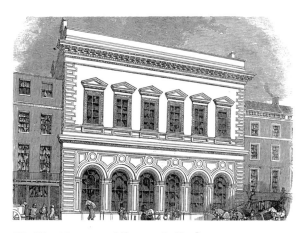

IX 26 *Museum of Economic Geology,*
London. By Sir James Pennethorne,
(c.1845) 1847–48 (1851). Jermyn St. entrance.

IX 27 *Museum of Economic Geology.*
Piccadilly front.

IX 28 *Museum of Economic Geology.*
Details of iron roof construction.

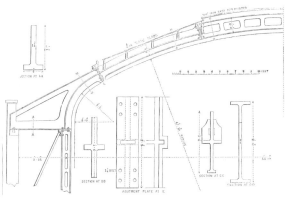

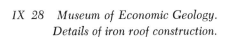

IX 29   *Museum of Economic Geology. Gallery.*

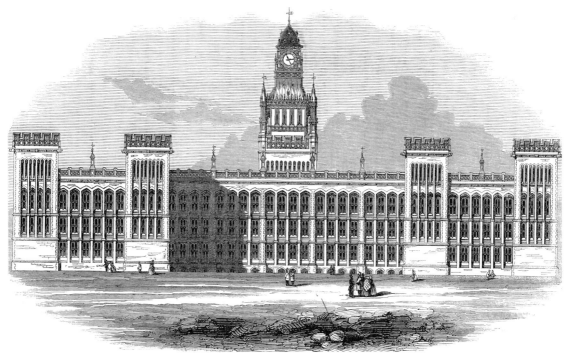

IX 30   *Record Office, Chancery Lane, London. By Sir James Pennethorne. The north front as projected, 1851.*

IX 31   *Ordnance Office, London. By Sir James Pennethorne, 1850–51. Pall Mall front.*

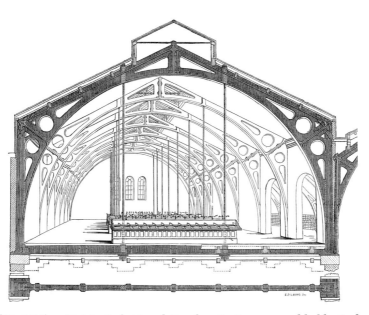

IX 32   *General Post Office, St. Martin-le-Grand, London. Sorting room added by Sydney Smirke, 1845.*

X CORPORATE ARCHITECTURE

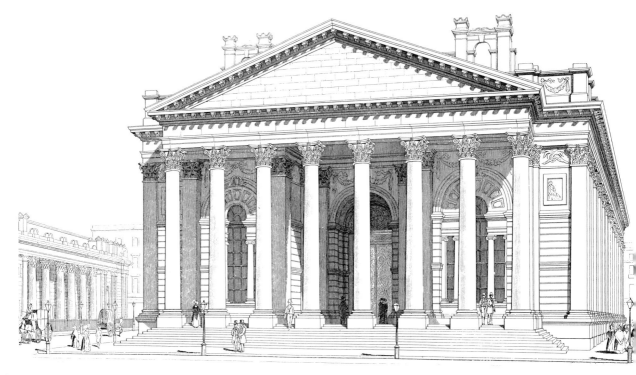

X 1   The Royal Exchange, London. By Sir William Tite, (1839) 1840–44. West front.

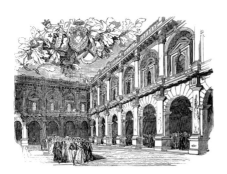

X 2   South front.

X 3   The court, with Royal
procession at the opening.

X 4   South and east fronts.

X 5   *Fitzwilliam Museum, Trumpington St., Cambridge. By George Basevi and C. R. Cockerell, 1837–47.*

X 6   *St. George's Hall, Lime St., Liverpool.*
By H. L. Elmes, Sir Robert Rawlinson, and C. R. Cockerell, (1839–40) 1841–54. East front.

X 7   *St. George's Hall. Plan.*   X 8   *North end.*

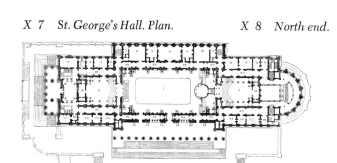

X 9 *University Galleries and Taylor Institute (Ashmolean), Beaumont and St. Giles Sts., Oxford. By C. R. Cockerell, (1840) 1841–45. Elevation toward Beaumont St.*

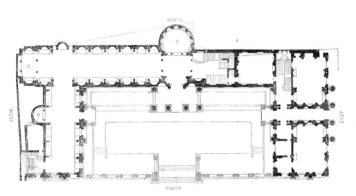

X 10 *University Galleries and Taylor Institute. Plan.*

X 11 *East front.*

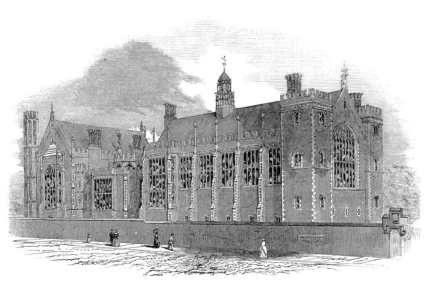

X 12 *Hall and Library of Lincoln's Inn, London. By Philip and P. C. Hardwick, 1843–45. West front.*

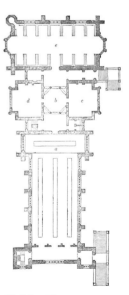

X 13 *Plan.*

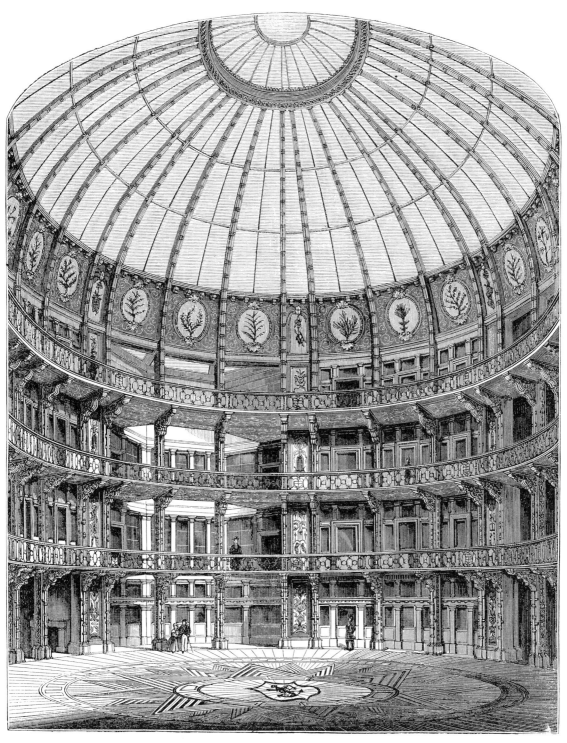

X 14   Coal Exchange, Lower Thames St., London. By J. B. Bunning, 1846–49. The court.

X 15   Coal Exchange. From the southeast.

X 16   Perspective.

X 17   Dome panels of tree ferns
designed by Melhado and executed by Sang.

X 18   Colliery in panel
painted by Sang.

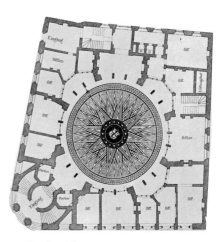

X 19   Plan.

X 20   "Jolly Miner" in panel
painted by Sang.

X 21   Coal Exchange. Dome ribs.

X 22   Second-storey stanchions.

X 23   Ground-storey stanchions.

X 24   First-storey stanchions.

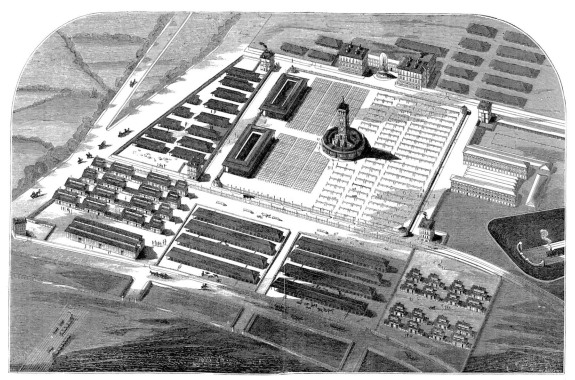

X 25   *Metropolitan Cattle Market*
(Caledonian Market), Copenhagen Fields, London. By J. B. Bunning, 1850–54.

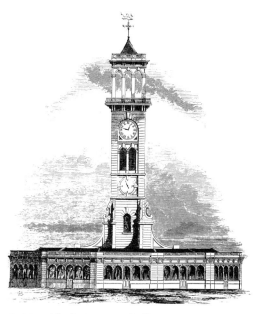

X 26   *Clock Tower and offices.*

X 27   *White Horse Tavern.*

X 28   Billingsgate Market, Lower Thames St., London. By J. B. Bunning, 1850–52.

X 29   Corn Exchange, Grass Market,
Edinburgh. By David Cousin, 1847–49.
Front and interior.

X 30   Town Hall and Market,
Truro, Cornwall. By Christopher
Eales, 1845–46. Front and rear.

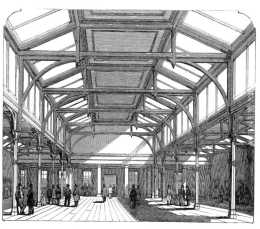

X 31 *Custom House, Ipswich.*
By J. M. Clark, 1843–45.

X 32 *St. Martin's Hall, Long Acre,*
London. By William Westmacott, 1847–50.

X 33 *Royal Academy Gold Medal project for a "Wellington College." By R. N. Shaw, 1853.*

X 34 *Wellington College, Sandhurst, Berkshire. Original design by John Shaw II, 1855.*

X 35   *Kneller Hall Training School, Whitton, Middlesex. By George Mair, 1848–50.*

X 36   *St. George's Hall, Bradford. By Lockwood and Mawson, 1851–53. Side and rear.*

X 37 St. George's Hall,
Lime St., Liverpool.
By H. L. Elmes, Robert Rawlinson,
and C. R. Cockerell,
(1839–40) 1841–47, 1847–49, 1851–54.
Opening of Great Hall.

X 38 Concert Room,
St. George's Hall.
By C. R. Cockerell, 1851–56.

X 39   *Concert Room, St. George's Hall. Stage.*

X 40 *National Gallery of Scotland, Edinburgh. By W. H. Playfair, 1850–54. (With the Royal Scottish Institution, 1822–36, on the right, and the Free Church College, 1846–50, behind; both also by Playfair.)*

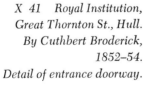

X 41 *Royal Institution,*
Great Thornton St., Hull.
By Cuthbert Broderick,
1852–54.
Detail of entrance doorway.

XI BANKS AND INSURANCE BUILDINGS

XI 1   Bank Chambers, 3 Cook St., Liverpool. By C. R. Cockerell, 1849–50.

XI 2   London and Westminster Bank, London. By C. R. Cockerell, 1837–38. Original façade.

XI 3   Legal and General Life Assurance Office, London. By Thomas Hopper, c.1838. (On the right.) Center building by George Aitchison I, c.1855.

XI 4 Sun Fire and Life Assurance Offices, Bartholomew Lane and
Threadneedle St., London. By C. R. Cockerell, (1839) 1840–42.

XI 5 Liverpool and London Insurance
Offices, Dale St. and Exchange Pl.,
Liverpool. By C. R. Cockerell, 1856–58.

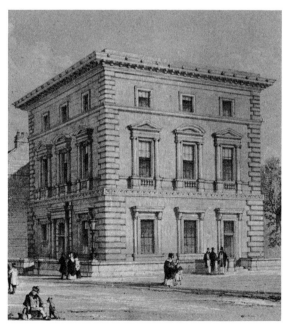

XI 6 Savings Bank, Bath.
By George Alexander, 1840–41.

XI 7   Commercial Bank of Scotland,
George St., Edinburgh.
By David Rhind, 1844–46.

XI 9   Branch Bank of England. Castle and Cook
Sts., Liverpool. By C. R. Cockerell, 1845–58.
Front and side.

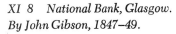

XI 8   National Bank, Glasgow.
By John Gibson, 1847–49.

XI 10 Branch Bank of England, Broad St., Bristol. By C. R. Cockerell, 1844–46.

XI 11 *Stanley Dock, Liverpool. By Jesse Hartley, 1852–56. Warehouses after blitz.*

XI 12 *Royal Insurance Buildings,*
Liverpool. By William Grellier, 1846–49.

XI 13 *Stanley Dock.*
Walls and entrances.

XI 14   *Imperial Assurance Office,*
London.
By John Gibson, 1846–48.

XI 15   *Queen's Assurance and Commercial*
Chambers, 42–44 Gresham St., London.
By Sancton Wood, 1851–52.

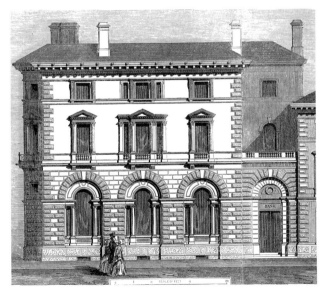

XI 16   *Sir Benjamin Heywood's Bank, St. Ann's Sq., Manchester.*
By J. E. Gregan, 1848–49. St. Ann's St. elevation (left) and entrance (right).

XI 17 Corn Exchange (left) and Bank (right), Market Sq., Northampton.
By George Alexander and Hall, (1849) 1850–51, and E. F. Law, 1850, respectively.

 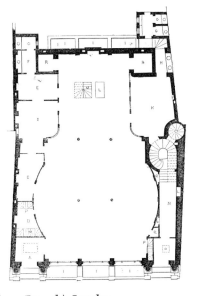

XI 18 London and Westminster Bank (Bloomsbury Branch), London.
By Henry Baker, 1853–54. Elevation and plan.

XII   COMMERCIAL STREET ARCHITECTURE

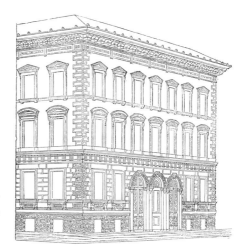

XII 1   *Brunswick Buildings, Liverpool.*
By A. and G. Williams, 1841–42.

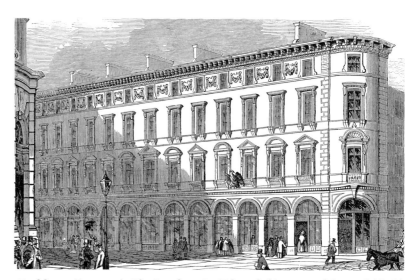

XII 2   *Royal Exchange Buildings, Freeman's Pl., London. By Edward l'Anson and Son, 1844–45.*

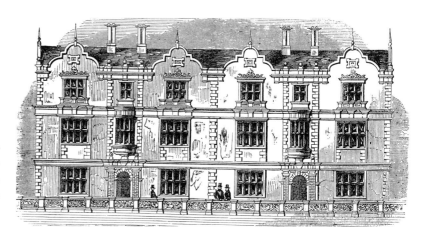

XII 3   *Chambers,*
Staple Inn, London.
By Wigg and Pownall,
1842–43.

XII 4 Nos. 93–105
New Oxford St., London.
Possibly by Sir James
Pennethorne, c.1845–47.

XII 5 Faringdon St. North, London.
As intended to be completed, 1843.

XII 6 Block of shops, New Coventry St., London.
By Charles Mayhew, 1843–44.

XII 7 Nos. 44–50 New Oxford St.,
London. c.1845–47.

*XII 8   Nos. 75–77 New Oxford St., London.
Possibly by Sir James Pennethorne, c.1845–47.*

XII 9   Terrace of shops and houses, Queen St., Glasgow. By James Wylson, 1848.

*XII 10   Colonial Buildings,
Horse Fair and Windmill St.,
Birmingham. c.1845.*

XII 11   Nos. 5–9 Aldermanbury, London. c.1840?

XII 12   Boote Buildings,
Elliott St., Liverpool. 1846.

XII 13   No. 50 Watling St.,
London. c.1843?

XII 14   S. Schwabe Warehouse, 46–54 Mosley
St., Manchester. By Edward Walters, 1845.

XII 15   The Quadrant, Regent St., London.
By John Nash, 1819–20, but revised by Sir James Pennethorne, 1848.

XII 16   James Brown, Son, and Co. Warehouse,
9 Portland St., Manchester. By Edward Walters, 1851–52.

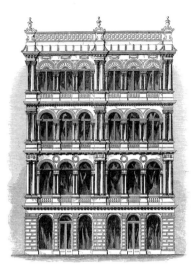

XII 17   Two shops in Market St., Manchester.
By Starkey and Cuffley, 1851.

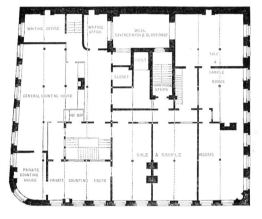

XII 18   Warehouse, Portland and Parker Sts.,
Manchester. By J. E. Gregan,
1850. Elevation and plan.

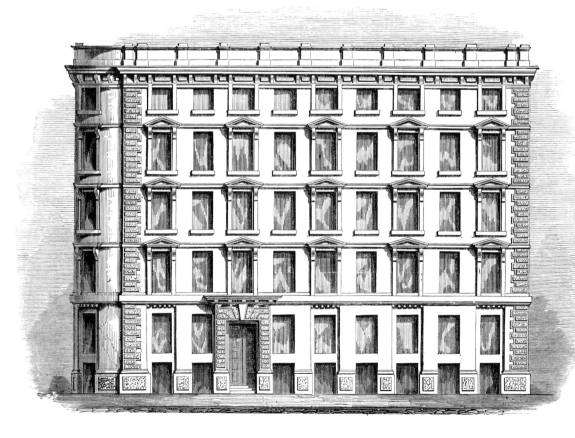

XII 19 *Shops and houses,*
New Oxford St., London.
By Henry Stansby, 1849.

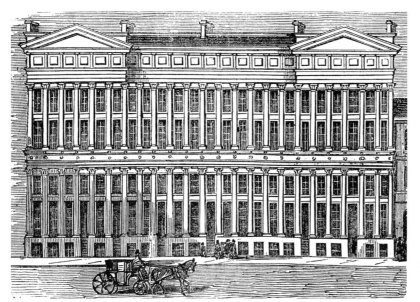

XII 20 *Warehouse in Mosley*
St., Manchester. Before 1851.

PLAY-GROUND

XII 21 *Northern Schools,*
St. Martin's-in-the-Fields,
Castle St., London.
By J. W. Wild, 1849–50.

 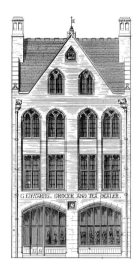 

XII 22   Mr. Fair's shop and
house, Prince's St., London, 1842.

XII 23   Project for grocer's shop.
By A. N. W. Pugin, 1843.

XII 24   Perfumery shopfront,
Piccadilly, London, 1850.

XII 25   Prefabricated shops and dwellings, Melbourne, Australia. Made by Samuel Hemming in Bristol, 1853.

XII 26   L. T. Piver shopfront,
160 Regent St., London. By Cambon, 1846.

XII 27   Shops in New Oxford St.,
London, 1851.

XII 28   Warehouse, 12 Temple St., Bristol. Perhaps by W. B. Gingell, c.1855.

XII 29   Nos. 188–192 Strand, London. By H. R. Abraham, 1852.

XIII THE BEGINNINGS OF VICTORIAN HOUSING

XIII 1 *Gloucester Sq.,
from Hyde Park Sq.,
Bayswater, London.
1837–c.1847.
Northwest side
being demol-
ished in 1936.*

XIII 2 *Milner Sq.,
Islington, London.
By Gough and
Roumieu, 1841–43.
(Photo Country Life.)*

XIII 3 *Lonsdale Sq.,
Islington, London.
Begun by R. C.
Carpenter in 1838.
(Photo Country Life.)*

XIII 4 *Royal Promenade,*
Victoria Sq., Clifton.
Begun 1837.

XIII 5 *Worcester Terrace,*
Clifton. Completed 1851–53
from earlier design.

XIII 6 *Gloucester Sq., Bayswater,*
London. Southeast side, c.1840–45.

XIII 7 *Lansdowne Place, Plymouth.*
Probably by George Wightwick, c.1845.

XIII 8 Nos. 4–8
Eastgate St.,
Winchester. c.1840.

XIII 9 Nos. 10–20
Eastgate St.,
Winchester. c.1840.

XIII 10 Peacock Terrace,
Liverpool Grove,
Walworth, London. 1842.

XIII 11   *"Grecian Villa."*
By S. H. Brooks, 1839.

XIII 12   *Semidetached "second-rate" houses.*
T. L. Walker's Architectural Precedents, *1841.*

XIII 13   *"Villa in the Florentine Style." By Richard Brown, 1842.*

XIII 14 *National School for 500 children. By Charles Parker, 1841.*

XIII 15 *"Villa in the Italian Style." By John White, 1845.*

XIII 16　Jacobethan entrance. By John White, 1845.

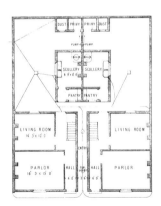

XIII 17　£200 row houses. By Samuel Hemming, c.1855. Elevation and plan.

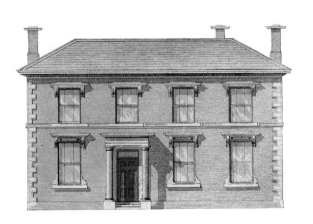

XIII 18　£670 parsonage house. By Samuel Hemming, c.1855. Elevation and plan.

XIII 19   Semidetached £750 houses. By Samuel Hemming, c.1855.

XIII 20   Terrace, Lowndes Sq., Belgravia, London. By Lewis Cubitt, 1841–43. Elevation and plans of corner house.

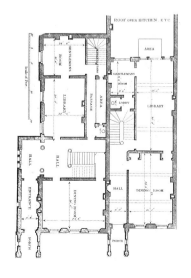

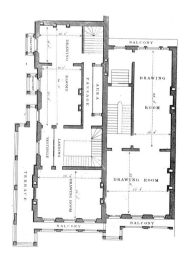

XIII 21   Lyppiat Terrace, Cheltenham. Probably by R. W. Jearrad, c.1845.

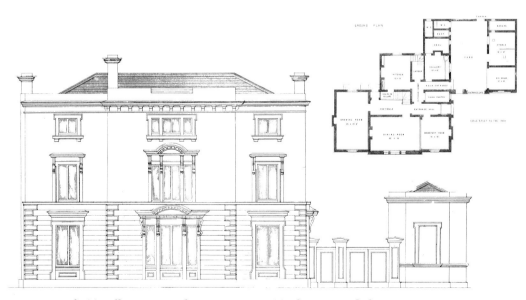

XIII 22   £1550 villa. By Samuel Hemming, c.1855. Elevation and plan.

XIII 23   Terrace, Westbourne Terrace, Paddington, London. Probably by R. P. Browne, c.1845.

XIII 24   Westbourne Terrace. c.1845.

XIII 25   Quasi-semidetached houses, Westbourne Terrace. Probably by R. P. Browne, c.1845–50.

XIII 26   Gloucester Crescent, Camden Town, London. c.1850.

XIII 27   Kensington Gate, Gloucester Rd., London. Probably by Bean, c.1850.

XIII 28   Quasi-semidetached houses, Gloucester Terrace, Paddington, London. c.1845–50.

XIII 29   College Terrace,
Stepney, London.
c.1845–50.

XIII 30   Llandudno, North Wales. By Wehnert and Ashdown (and others), 1849–55.

XIII 31   St. Ann's
Villas, Norland Rd.,
London. c.1847.

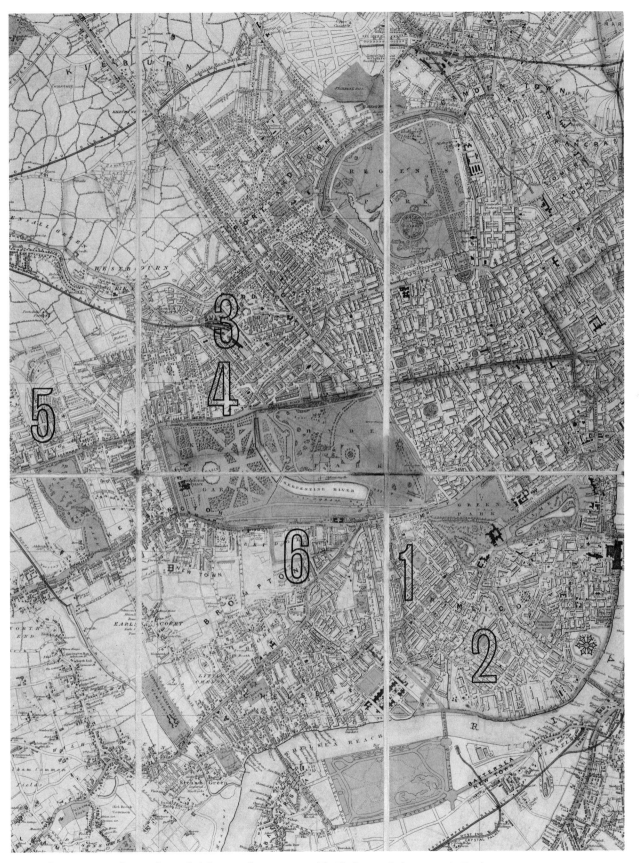

XIII 32   *West London in the mid-50's. Map by James Wyld, 1858.   1. Belgravia   2. Pimlico*
3. Paddington   4. Bayswater   5. Ladbroke Grove   6. Commissioners' Estate

XIII 33 *Blenheim Mount, Manningham Lane, Bradford. c.1855.*

XIII 34 *Terrace with shops below,*
St. George's Place, Knightsbridge, London. By F. R. Beeston, c.1848.

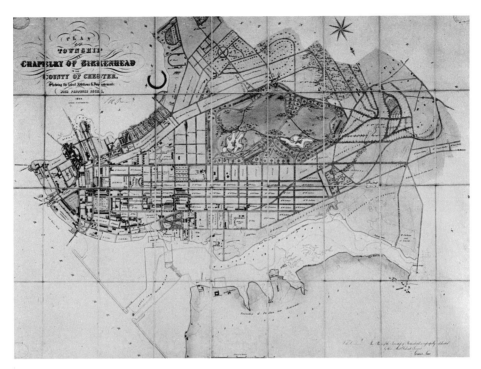

XIII 35   *Plan of Birkenhead in 1844, with proposed docks.*

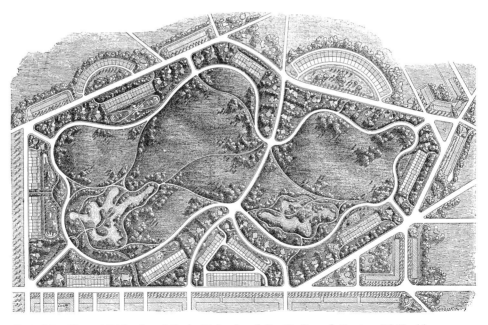

XIII 36   *Plan of Birkenhead Park, Birkenhead. By Sir Joseph Paxton, 1842–44.*

XIII 37 *Semidetached houses,*
39–41 White Ladies Road, Clifton. c.1855.

XIII 38 *Birkenhead Park Lodge,*
88 Park Rd. South, Birkenhead.
By Lewis Hornblower, 1844.

XIV HOUSING IN THE MID-CENTURY

XIV 1 *Gloucester Arms*
public house and contiguous
houses, Gloucester Terrace,
Paddington, London. c.1852.

XIV 2 *Salt Mill,*
Saltaire, near Bradford,
Yorkshire. By Lockwood
and Mawson, and Sir
William Fairbairn, 1851–53.
General view.

XIV 3 *Salt Mill.*
Entrance to offices.

XIV 4   Model Lodging House
for Single Men, George St.,
St. Giles, London.
By Henry Roberts, 1846–47.

XIV 5   Model Lodging Houses,
Clerkenwell, London.
By Henry Roberts, 1845–46.
Perspective and plans.

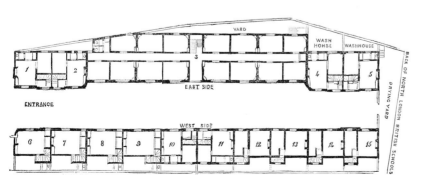

XIV 6 Model Houses for Families (flatted),
Streatham and George Sts., Bloomsbury,
London. By Henry Roberts, 1849–50. Exterior.

XIV 7 Access galleries in court.

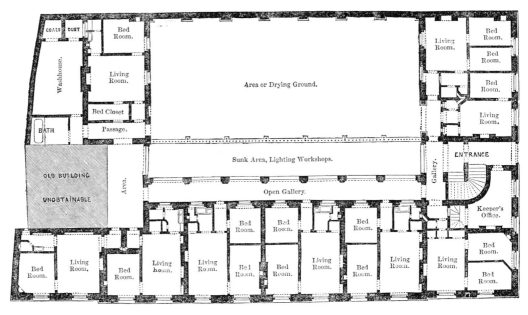

XIV 8 Plan of ground floor.

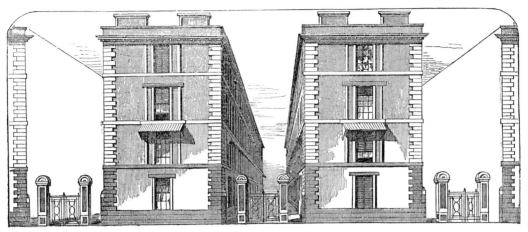

XIV 9   Workmen's Dwellings (flatted), Birkenhead. 1845–46.

XIV 10   Project for Model Town Houses for the Middle Classes (flatted). By William Young, 1849. Perspective and plans.

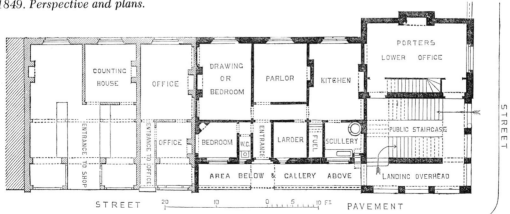

XIV 11 *Apartment houses in Victoria St. between Carlisle Pl. and Howick Pl. By Henry Ashton, 1852–54. General view looking east.*

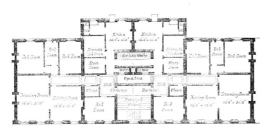

XIV 12 *Typical upper-floor plan of one "house" with two apartments opening on one stair.*

XIV 13 *Terrace, Woodhouse Sq., Leeds. c.1850–55.*

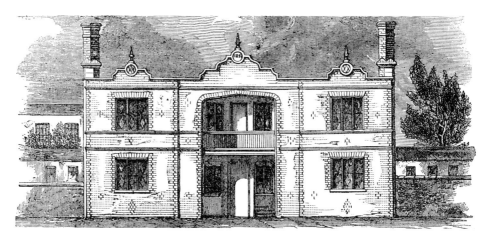

XIV 14 *Prince Albert's Model Houses, Hyde Park, London (now in Kennington Park). By Henry Roberts, 1850–51.*

XIV 15 Prince's Gate, Kensington Rd., London. By Johnston, 1850–51. Front and rear elevations.

XIV 16 Nos. 70–74 Eastgate St., Winchester. c.1850.

XIV 17 St. Aidan's Terrace, Forest Rd., Birkenhead. Possibly by T. H. Wyatt, c.1853.

XIV 18   South side of Grosvenor Sq., London. Three houses have Early Victorian fronts, all probably by Thomas Cundy II, c.1855.

XIV 19   Terrace, Hyde Park Sq., Bayswater, London. c.1840.

XIV 20   Terrace between Cleveland S[...] and Cleveland Gardens, Paddington, London. c.1850–55. Entrance front.

XIV 21 *Terrace, Moray Place, Strathbungo, Glasgow. By Alexander Thomson, 1860.*

XIV 22 *Terrace between Cleveland Sq. and Cleveland Gardens, Paddington, London. c.1850–55. Garden front.*

XIV 23 *Terrace, Victoria Sq., Clifton. c.1855.*

XIV 24 Walmer Crescent,
Paisley Rd., Glasgow.
By Alexander Thomson, 1858.

XIV 25 Queen's Park Terrace
(flatted), Eglinton Street,
Glasgow. By Alexander Thomson,
1859.

XV EARLY RAILWAY STATIONS

AND OTHER IRON CONSTRUCTION

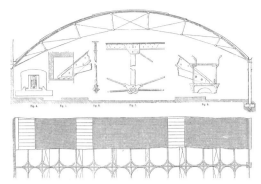

XV 1   *Lime St. I Railway Station, Liverpool.*
By John Cunningham, opened in 1836. Shed.

XV 2   *Lime St. II Railway Station. Shed by*
Richard Turner, 1849–51. Plan and section.

XV 3   *Lime St. I Railway Station, Liverpool. Entrance Screen by John Foster, completed 1836.*

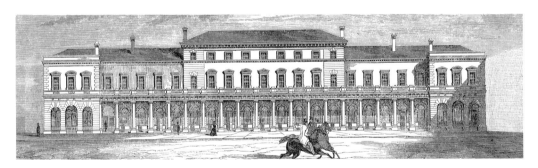

XV 4   *Lime St. II Railway Station, Liverpool. Station block facing Lord Nelson St.*
by Sir William Tite, 1846–50. Elevation.   XV 5   Plan.

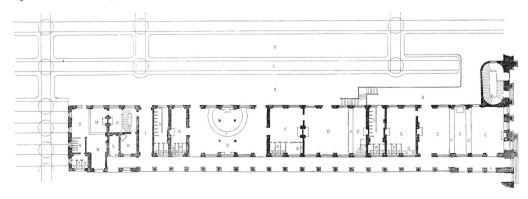

XV 6   Euston I Railway Station, London. The "Arch" by Philip Hardwick, 1835–37.

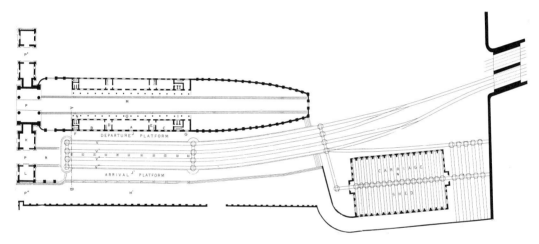

XV 7   Plan of Euston I Railway Station. By Robert Stephenson and Philip Hardwick, 1835–39.

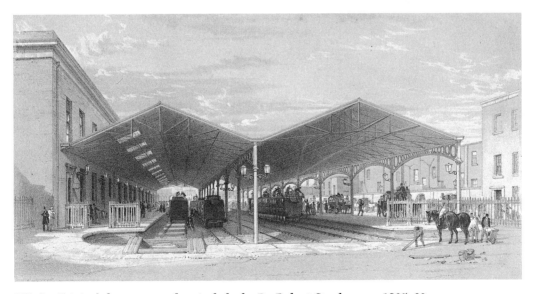

XV 8   Original departure and arrival sheds. By Robert Stephenson, 1835–39.

XV 9 *Projects for bridges on the "Antient Principles," with stations. By A. N. W. Pugin, 1843.*

XV 10 *Nine Elms Railway Station (now Transport Museum), Vauxhall, London. By Joseph Locke and Sir William Tite, 1837–38.*

XV 11   *Trijunct Railway Station and North Midland Station Hotel, Derby.
By Robert Stephenson and Francis Thompson, 1839–41.*

XV 12   *Trijunct Railway Station, Derby. Sheds.*

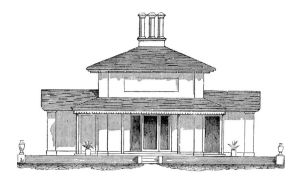

XV 13 and 14   *Railway stations at Wingfield and Ambergate, Derbyshire. By Francis Thompson,
c.1840. "Revised to serve as cottage residences," by J. C. Loudon, 1842.*

XV 15   Paddington I Railway Station, under Bishop's Rd., London. By I. K. Brunel, 1838.

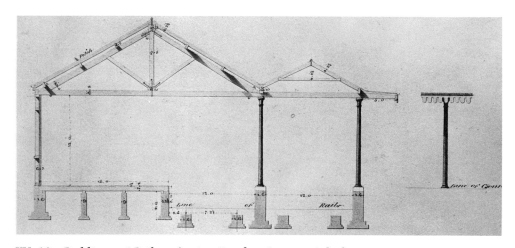

XV 16   Paddington I Railway Station, London. Section of shed.

XV 17   Clifton Suspension Bridge, Clifton Gorge.
Designed and begun by I. K. Brunel, and finished by W. H. Barlow, (1829) 1837–63.

XV 18 *The Queen's Hotel, Cheltenham.*
By R. W. Jearrad, opened in 1837.

XV 19 *Great Western Hotel,*
Bristol. By R. S. Pope, opened in 1839.

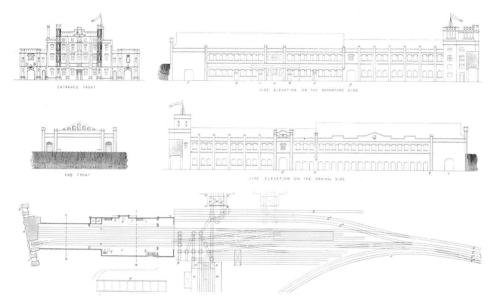

XV 20 *Temple Mead I Railway Station, Bristol. By I. K. Brunel, 1839–40. Plan and elevations.*

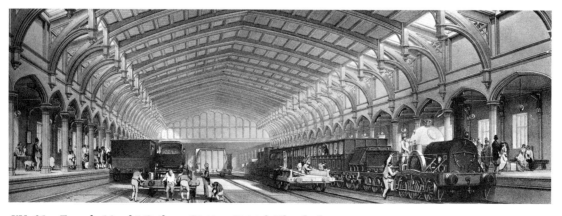

XV 21 *Temple Mead I Railway Station, Bristol. The shed.*

XV 22 Great Northern Railway Station,
Tanner Row, York. By T. G. Andrews, 1840–42. The triple shed, with the Queen entraining.

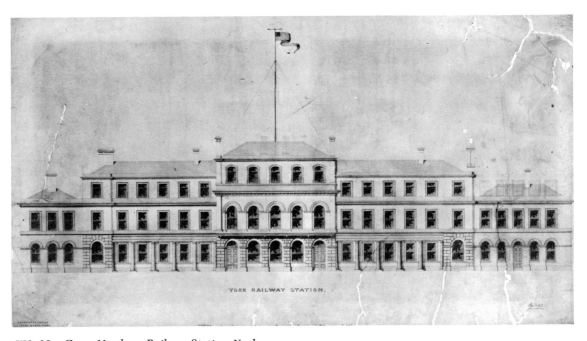

XV 23 Great Northern Railway Station, York.
Departure-side elevation, with added storey for hotel accommodation indicated over head-block to right.

XV 24 *South-Eastern Railway Station, Bricklayers' Arms,*
Southwark, London. By Lewis Cubitt, 1842–44. Entrance screen.

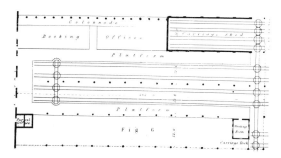

XV 25 *South-Eastern Railway Station,*
Bricklayers' Arms. Plan.

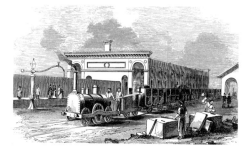

XV 26 *Eastern Counties Railway Station,*
Cambridge. By Sancton Wood, 1844–45.

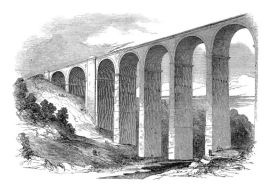

XV 27 *Congleton Viaduct, North Staffordshire*
Railway. By J. C. Forsyth, opened in 1849.

XV 28 *Croydon and Epsom Atmospheric Railway*
Station, Epsom. By J. R. and J. A. Brandon, 1844–45.

XV 29   Great Conservatory, Chatsworth. By Sir Joseph Paxton and Decimus Burton, (1836) 1837–40. (Photo Country Life)

XV 30   King Eyambo's Palace, Calabar River, Africa. Prefabricated by John Walker in London, 1843–44.

XV 31   Palm Stove, Royal Botanic Gardens, Kew. By Decimus Burton and Richard Turner, 1845–47. Exterior.

XV 32 and 33   Palm Stove, Kew. Interior, section, and details.

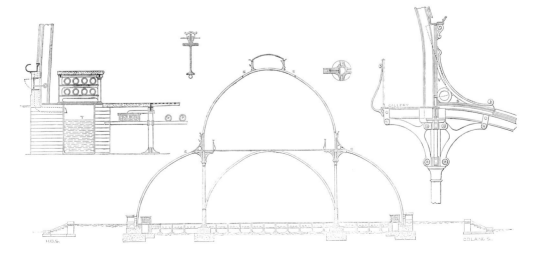

XV 34 *Britannia Bridge, Menai Strait, Wales. By Robert Stephenson and Francis Thompson, 1845–50.*
(The Menai Bridge in the distance is by Thomas Telford, 1819–24.)

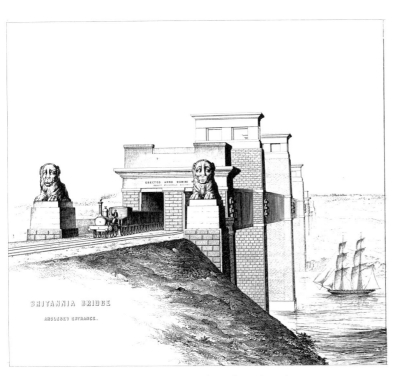

XV 35 *The Anglesey entrance, with lions by John Thomas.*

XV 36 *Section of tube.*

XV 37 Tubular Bridge, Conway, Wales. By Robert Stephenson and Francis Thompson, 1845–49. Floating the second tube into position to be hoisted.

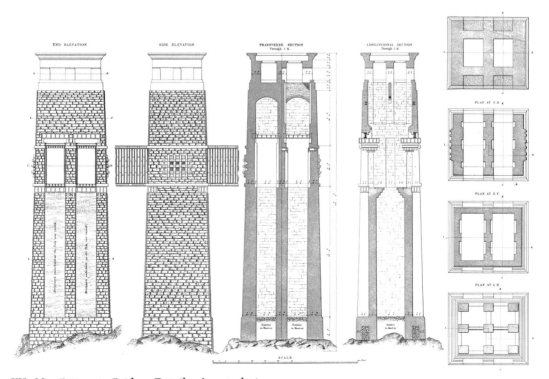

XV 38 Britannia Bridge. Details of central pier.

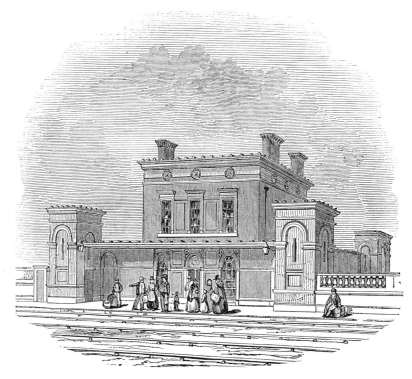

XV 39 Chester and Holyhead Railway Station, Holywell, Wales. By Francis Thompson, 1847–48.

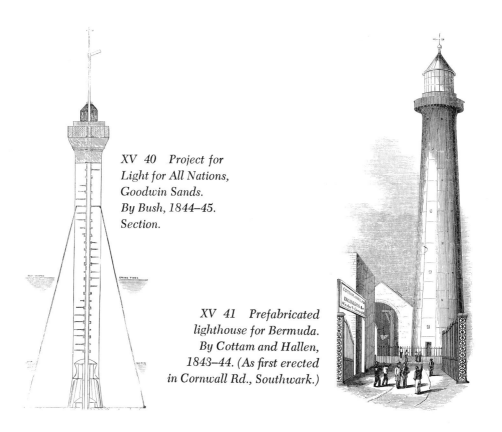

XV 40 Project for Light for All Nations, Goodwin Sands. By Bush, 1844–45. Section.

XV 41 Prefabricated lighthouse for Bermuda. By Cottam and Hallen, 1843–44. (As first erected in Cornwall Rd., Southwark.)

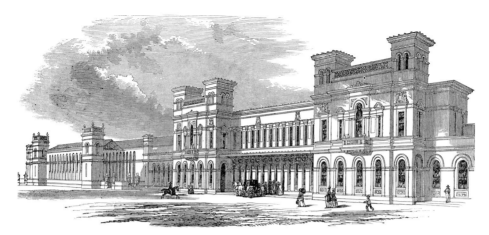

XV 42   *General Station, Chester. By Robert Stephenson and Francis Thompson, 1844–48.*

XV 43   *General Station, Chester. Sheds.*

XV 44   *Paragon Railway Station Hotel, Hull. By T. G. Andrews, 1847–48. Queen Victoria arriving.*

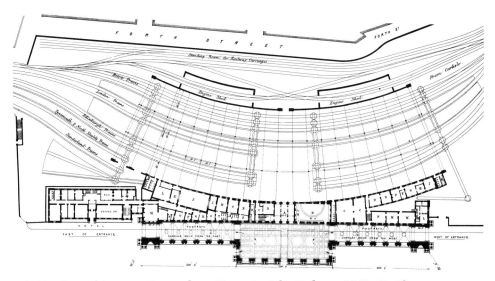

XV 45   *Central Station, Newcastle-on-Tyne. By John Dobson, 1846–50. Plan.*

XV 46   *Central Station, Newcastle-on-Tyne. The sheds.*

XV 47   *Shoreditch II Railway Station, London. By Sancton Wood, 1848–49. The sheds.*

XV 48   Sailors' Home, Canning Pl., Liverpool.
By John Cunningham, 1846–49. Section showing cast-iron galleries in court.

XV 49   Euston II Railway Station, London.
By P. C. Hardwick, 1846–49. Great Hall.

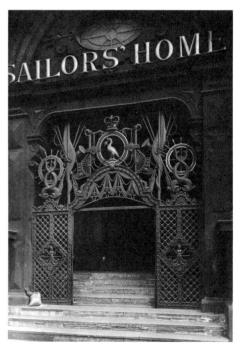

XV 50   Sailors' Home, Liverpool.
Entrance gates.

XV 51 *Prefabricated buildings*
awaiting shipment at Samuel Hemming's Clift-House Iron Building Works near Bristol in 1854.

XV 52 *Prefabricated iron and glazed*
terra cotta clock tower for Geelong,
Australia. By James Edmeston, 1854.

XV 53 *Prefabricated iron warehouse, with living rooms*
above, for export to San Francisco. By E. T. Bellhouse, 1850.

XV 54 *Prefabricated iron ballroom, Balmoral Castle,*
near Ballater, Fifeshire. By E. T. Bellhouse, 1851.

XVI THE CRYSTAL PALACE:

FERRO-VITREOUS TRIUMPH

AND ENSUING REACTION

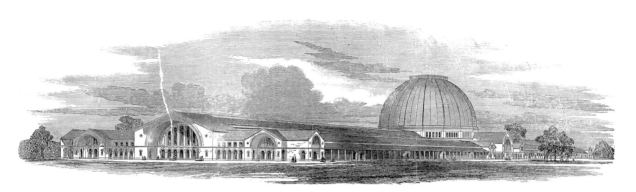

XVI 1   Official Design for the Edifice for the Great Exhibition of 1851. By Building Committee of Royal Commission, 1850. From Illustrated London News, 22 June 1850.

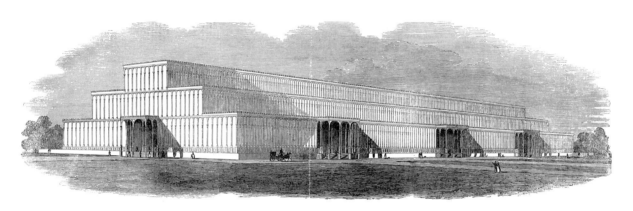

XVI 2   First developed design for Crystal Palace I. By Sir Joseph Paxton, June 1850. As published in Illustrated London News, 6 July 1850.

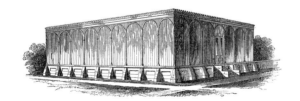 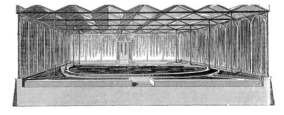

XVI 3   Lily House, Chatsworth, Derbyshire. By Sir Joseph Paxton, 1849–50. Perspective and section.

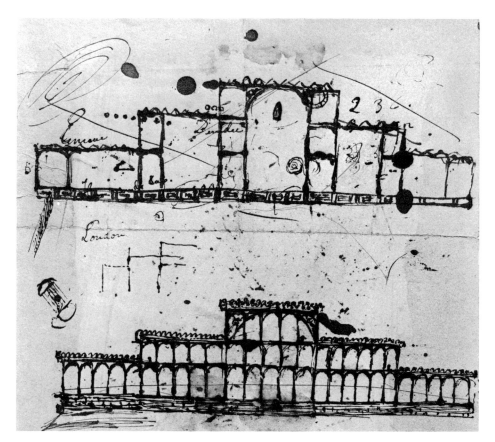

XVI 4 *Original sketch for Crystal Palace. By Sir Joseph Paxton, middle of June 1850.*

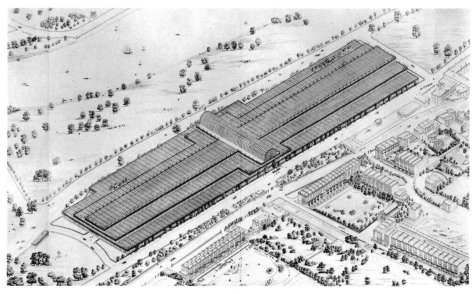

XVI 5 *Crystal Palace I, Hyde Park, London.*
By Sir Joseph Paxton, and Fox and Henderson, 1 August 1850–1 May 1851. Birdseye view.

XVI 6   *Crystal Palace, Hyde Park,*
London. By Sir Joseph Paxton, and Fox and Henderson, 1850–51. End view.

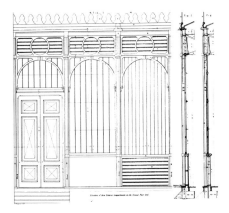

XVI 7   *Standard*
bay elevation.

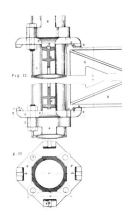

XVI 8   *Details of*
stanchions and girders.

XVI 9   *Looking across the nave at gallery level.*

XVI 10   *Midland Station, Park End St., Oxford. By Fox and Henderson, 1851–52. Entrance porch and sheds.*

XVI 11   Sash-bar machine used at site during erection of Crystal Palace I, Hyde Park, London.

XVI 12   Early stage in construction of Crystal Palace I. October 1850.

XVI 13   Preparation of sub-assemblies at site for Crystal Palace I. November 1850.

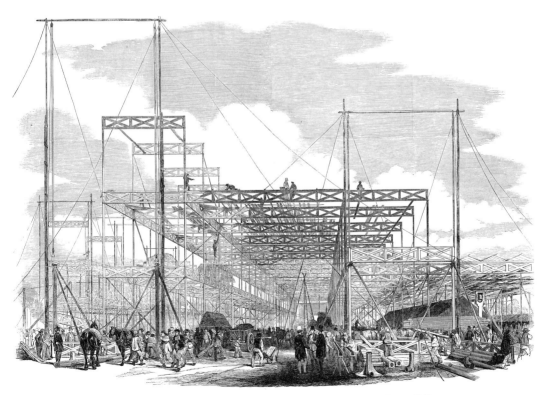

XVI 14   Crystal Palace I in construction. November 1850.

XVI 15   *Crystal Palace I, Hyde Park, London. By Sir Joseph Paxton, and Fox and Henderson,*
1 August 1850–1 May 1851. Transept with Sibthorp Elm.

XVI 16   *Nave before installation of exhibits. January 1851.*

XVI 17   Project for roofing court of Royal Exchange, London. By Sir Joseph Paxton, 1851.

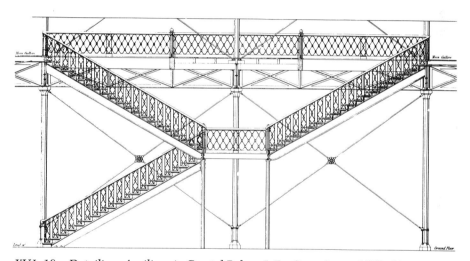

XVI 18   Detailing of railings in Crystal Palace I. By Owen Jones, 1850–51.

XVI 19   Project for New York Crystal Palace. By Sir Joseph Paxton, 1852.

XVI 20   *Project for reconstruction of Crystal Palace at Sydenham. By Sir Joseph Paxton, 1852.*

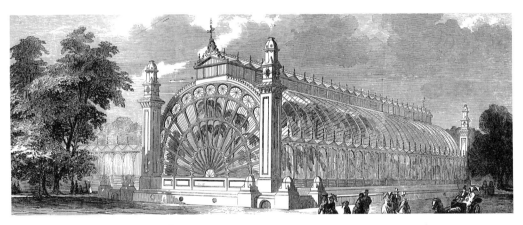

XVI 21   *Project for Exercise-Room,*
London Hospital for Diseases of the Chest, Victoria Park, London. By Sir Joseph Paxton, 1851.

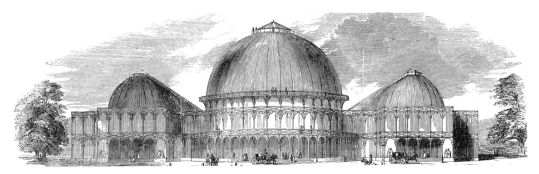

XVI 22   *Crystal Palace, Dublin. By Sir John Benson, 1852–53. Exterior.*

XVI 23   *Crystal Palace, Dublin. Interior.*

XVI 24   Crystal Palace II, Sydenham. By Sir Joseph Paxton,
and Fox, Henderson and Co., 1852–54. Exterior.

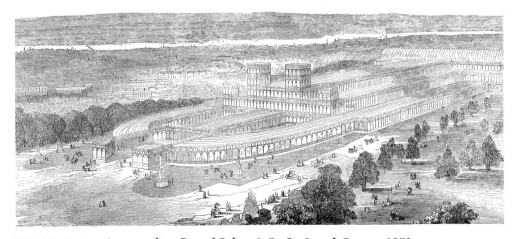

XVI 25   Project for extending Crystal Palace I. By Sir Joseph Paxton, 1852.

XVI 26 Crystal Palace II, Sydenham. By Sir Joseph Paxton, and Fox, Henderson and Co., 1852–54. Interior.

XVI 27   *Lord Warden Railway Hotel, Dover. By Samuel Beazley, 1850–53.*

XVI 28   *Southerndown Hotel, near Bridgend, Glamorganshire.*
By J. P. Seddon, 1852–53.

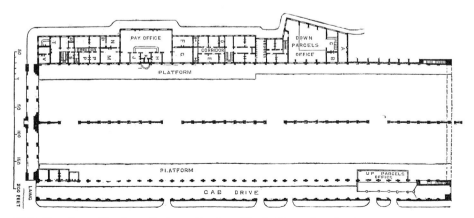

XVI 29   *Great Northern Railway Station, King's Cross, London.*
By Lewis Cubitt, (1850) 1851–52. Plan.

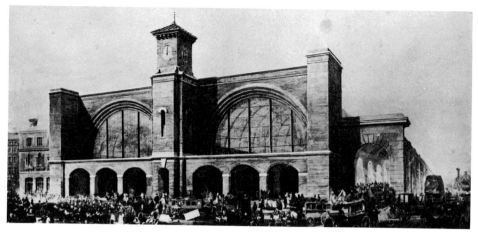

XVI 30   *King's Cross Railway Station, London. By Lewis Cubitt,*
(1850) 1851–52. Front of sheds on day of opening, 14 October 1852.

XVI 31   *Section of sheds.*

XVI 32   *Front of sheds today.*

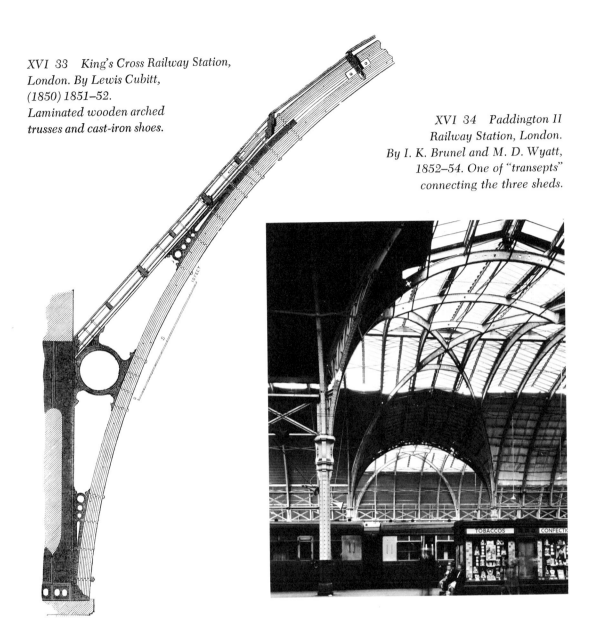

XVI 33 King's Cross Railway Station,
London. By Lewis Cubitt,
(1850) 1851–52.
Laminated wooden arched
trusses and cast-iron shoes.

XVI 34 Paddington II
Railway Station, London.
By I. K. Brunel and M. D. Wyatt,
1852–54. One of "transepts"
connecting the three sheds.

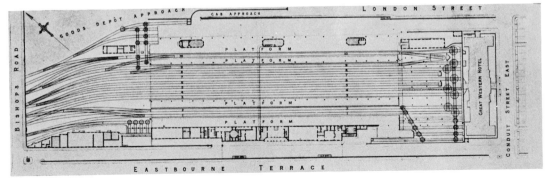

XVI 35 Paddington II Railway Station, London. Original plan.

XVI 36 *Paddington II. Sheds.*

XVI 37 *Paddington II. Interior wall of station block.*

XVI 38 "The Railway Station." By William P. Frith, 1861.

XVI 39 Paddington II. Stationmaster's oriel.

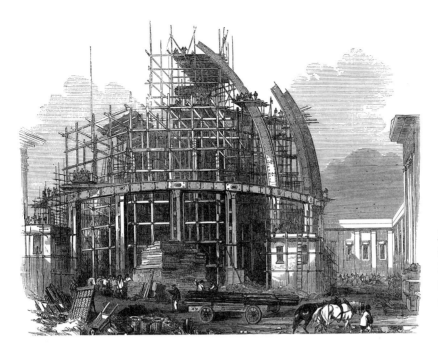

XVI 40 *British Museum,
Great Russell St., London.
Reading Room by Sydney
Smirke in construction
(1852) 1854–57.*

XVI 41 *Reading Room.
Interior.*

XVI 42 "The Aerial Ballet
of the Brompton Boilermakers."
(The Museum of Science
and Art, Brompton Park,
London, by Young and Son,
in construction, 1855–56.)

XVI 43 Museum of Science
and Art. Sidewalls in construction.

XVI 44 Museum of Science
and Art. Roof in construction.

XVI 45   *Museum of Science and Art. Galleries before completion.*

XVI 46   *Interior at official opening.*

XVI 47   *Museum of Science and Art, London. By Young and Son, 1855–56. Entrance porch.*

XVII RUSKIN OR BUTTERFIELD?

VICTORIAN GOTHIC AT THE MID-CENTURY

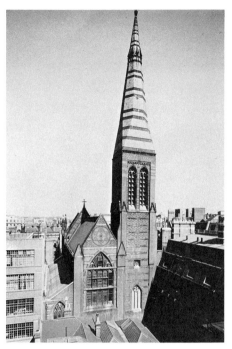

XVII 1   All Saints', Margaret St., Regent
St., London. William Butterfield, (1849)
1850–(1852)–1859. West front and tower.

XVII 2   First published
view of exterior, January 1853.

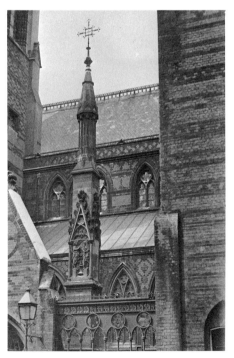

XVII 3   South
buttress with "Annunciation" relief.

XVII 4   Juxtaposition of south
porch, tower shaft, and choir school.

XVII 5   *All Saints', Margaret St., London. Interior.*

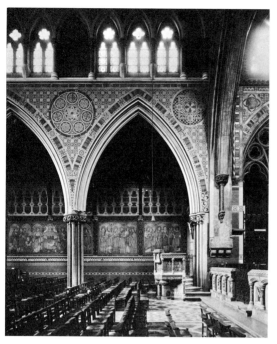

XVII 6 *All Saints', Margaret St., London.*
Nave arcade and chancel arch.

XVII 7 *South aisle.*

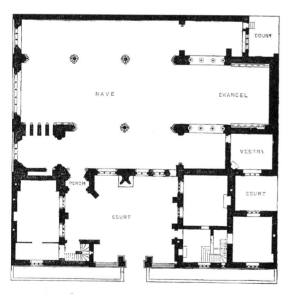

XVII 8 *Plan.*

XVII 9 *Interior looking east.*

XVII 10   *Choir School and Clergy House of All Saints', Margaret St.*

XVII 11   *All Saints', Margaret St. North wall of chancel.*

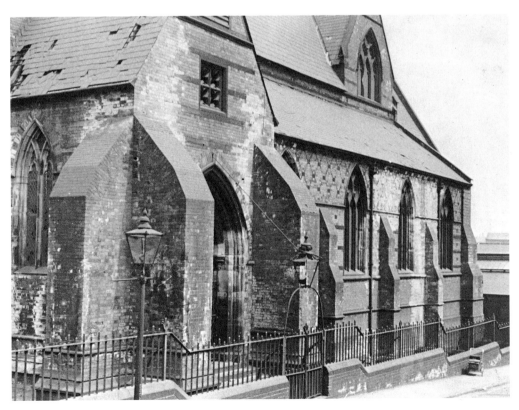

XVII 12   *St. Thomas's, Leeds. By William Butterfield, 1850–52.*

XVII 13   *Original project for St. Matthias's,*
Stoke Newington, London.
By William Butterfield, 1850.

XVII 14   *St. Matthias's, Howard Rd.,Stoke*
Newington, London. By William Butterfield,
(1850) 1851–53. The east end after blitz.

XVII 15   *West front after blitz.*